Generational
WEALTH

Why 90% Of Families Fail
To Establish A Lasting Legacy

A Dialogue Between
Two Family Wealth Experts
About How To Establish
Your Multi-Generational Family Legacy

Nicholas Charles and Antoaneta Proctor

Generational Wealth

Nicholas Charles & Antoaneta Proctor

First published in July 2022 by WM Publishing

ISBN 978-1-912774-96-8 ebk
ISBN 978-1-912774-97-5 hbk

Disclaimer: *Generational Wealth* is intended for information and education purposes only. This book does not constitute specific legal, financial, health, clinical, commercial or travel advice unique to your situation.

The views and opinions expressed in this book are those of the authors and do not reflect those of the Publisher and Resellers, who accept no responsibility for loss, damage or injury to persons or their belongings as a direct or indirect result of reading this book.

All people mentioned in case studies have been used with permission, and/or have had names, genders, industries and personal details altered to protect client confidentiality.

This book is dedicated to our families whose unconditional love has empowered and inspired us to be better every day.

Contents

Discover The Future
Of Generational Wealth With Danti.io

The insights and strategies outlined in Generational Wealth have sparked a profound shift in how we approach the protection and growth of family legacies. Inspired by the very principles within this book, Danti was born—a secure, cutting-edge platform designed to empower Ultra High Net Worth families to digitize, manage, and protect their wealth for generations to come.

At Danti, we take the complexities of multi-generational wealth planning and governance and bring them into the digital age. From safeguarding assets to seamless communication with trusted advisors, Danti offers a comprehensive solution tailored to the unique needs of family offices and wealth stewards. We are transforming the way families envision their legacies, making it easier than ever to preserve and grow wealth across generations.

Danti is not just a wealth management platform, it's the future of legacy building, a fully integrated, secure operating system designed specifically for family offices and Ultra High Net Worth individuals. What sets Danti apart is its unique approach to wealth management through a blueprint centered on the 10 Pillars of Generational Wealth: Vision, Health, Communication, Assets, Philanthropy, Advisors, Governance, Education, Documentation, and Structures.

Unfortunately, statistics show that 9 out of 10 families fail to preserve their wealth across generations. Danti is here to help families BE THE ONE that secures a lasting legacy, not the nine that fall short. By focusing on these key pillars, Danti provides a comprehensive and strategic foundation for building, maintaining, and growing generational wealth.

Danti's Agile approach is another factor that sets us apart. We continually test, learn, and adapt, ensuring that our strategy is tailored to the unique needs of each family.

While every family is different, they all share one common goal— preserving their wealth and legacy for future generations. Danti is dedicated to helping families achieve that goal, ensuring their legacy stands the test of time.

Don't leave your family's wealth to chance.

Visit *www.danti.io* to learn how Danti can help your family build a lasting legacy.

Introduction To Alexander Hoare

Nicholas Charles

*"There are two things that can destroy a family business:
the business and the family, and both have to be kept in order."*
Alexander Hoare

History is filled with stories of heirs who have lost their family fortunes. The old saying 'shirtsleeves to shirtsleeves within three generations' is borne out by studies that show more than 90% of families have failed to retain their family wealth for three generations.

There is a common perception that careful and well thought out estate planning is sufficient to secure a family's wealth and legacy. As a Chartered Certified Accountant and legacy advisor to high-net-worth families who is also the scion of a family that had generational wealth and lost it, I know that this perception is wrong.

I wrote this book to impact families and to change the dynamic of failure.

Wealth consists of more than just financial capital.

The main problem I have uncovered is that families do not understand or appreciate the real value of wealth.

Wealth does not consist of financial capital alone. It also includes human, intellectual, and social capital. The message to your children must be to create a destiny that moves your family into that rarity of multi-generational financial success. My mission from the outset was to create a paradigm shift in family legacy planning.

Having a family legacy that thrives for multiple generations can have a material impact on the planet. It is a worthy aspiration.

It all starts by creating a vision and purpose for the family wealth that is greater than the individual needs of each family member. It is essential that your family has a powerful and inspiring reason for retaining wealth for multiple generations otherwise it will never happen.

Successful families may have different backgrounds, business interests, and investments but they all have similar traits, systems, and values around family wealth. In fact, they all appreciate and understand what real wealth is and what is required to retain it for multiple generations.

This book studies families that have lost it all as well as those that have succeeded. It then details what is required to ensure your family does not end up becoming another damned statistic. We give concepts and principles for all families to incorporate into their thinking when it comes to establishing a legacy that thrives for multiple generations.

Whilst writing this book, I discovered a family whose story I found truly inspiring. They are very private but their family business, a private bank, was opened in 1672 and is still owned by the family today. Their story is amazing, especially when you realise that their business is one hundred years older than the Rothschild banking group. Their history and how they operate today, is a prime example of what needs to be done to create a business legacy that thrives for multiple generations.

The name of the private bank in question? C Hoare & Co.

It was evident to me that I had to reach out and speak with at least one member of the family board, as I wanted to know more about their success story.

So, I dusted down my Parker pen and sent each family board member a hand-addressed package with a personally signed copy of my first book along with a letter on my special metal embossed letterhead. I then waited, for a response, more in hope than expectation. Within just one week, I was amazed to receive a response from the office of Alexander Hoare himself, the last family member to be the CEO of the bank. Our call became an interview which then became the foreword to this book. It revealed some incredible insights as to what it takes to build a family dynasty that thrives in perpetuity.

I am honoured and grateful that Mr Hoare was kind enough to respond.

NICHOLAS CHARLES & ANTOANETA PROCTOR

Foreword By Alexander Hoare
Director – C. Hoare & Co Private Bank

When Nicholas Charles approached me for an interview about family wealth and how to maintain a successful business for multiple generations, I was intrigued. I am usually approached to discuss either finance, our private bank, C Hoare & Co, or both. However, Nicholas was more interested in the concept of the business of being a family rather than just how to achieve success in a family business. We discussed in detail the following quote that I stated in Bloomberg:

"There are two things that can destroy a family business: the business and the family, and both have to be kept in order."

It all starts with having a good business idea but there are only a small minority who are focused on the long term and want continuity. The cultural ambition is to get mega rich, buy a yacht and an aeroplane and this does not appeal to us. We enjoy our business which pays us well and keeps us very entertained. We are very good at what we do, and we focus on what we do best - to look after the banking needs of our customers. Whilst we do not have an advisory business, we are a relationship bank, and we talk with our customers. In fact, we want to ensure that our customers share our values, and we turn away a lot of people who do not share our values.

We sell, provide, and offer relationships which we hope will endure for a generation or more.

We are a values-driven business

The interview with Nicholas highlighted the fact that we are a values driven business which is one of the reasons why we have been in business since 1672. His book shares the importance of this concept and how understanding the values of each member of the family helps to facilitate better communication. Effective communication, or the lack of it, is the main reason why families fail to retain wealth for multiple generations. The family board communicates regularly about everything that is important surrounding the business. Occasionally, we even discuss selling the bank, but it always comes down to the same thing. Apart from getting a large pay-out from a sale, what would be the point? What else would we do? How would a sale make us happier?

It should be remembered that a lot of people die shortly after retirement. We love our work, so why remove the thing that continues to make us happy?

Family businesses are so unique in that each member must wear multiple 'hats.' We are directors, stakeholders and we are also family members. Juggling these various roles is a challenge but when you do it well the results are so much more rewarding than simply increasing the stock value of the company.

It is also essential that families have a vision so that they have a clear path for the future.

In our bank we have articulated a purpose statement 'to be good bankers and good citizens'. This purpose statement provides guidance on what we try to achieve with our bank. Whilst there are good banks and there are good citizens there are very few who try to be both.

It is fulfilling for us, to run a good business whilst giving a lot back to society and that is a great place to be.

One of the main reasons why our business has thrived is because of our collective desire to give back to society; to create a purpose greater than the individual needs of each family member. This comes via our sustainable philanthropic arm the Golden Bottle Trust. I really appreciate how Nicholas has summarised family prosperity with his *Four Fundamentals* formula. Unsurprisingly, we have applied the same formula to our business, but we started our successful family journey with sustainable philanthropy.

Sustainable philanthropy

This is one of the main reasons why I kept coming back to work for over three decades. The reason why we try to make the business better and more successful is the fact that we give away ten percent of our profits to charity. It acts like a double inspiration because just giving back is inspirational, but philanthropy is also great fun, and it can be a very good glue that keeps the family together, with all sorts of intangible benefits attached to it as well.

Our bank set up the Golden Bottle Trust which does various things. One of these is to double match whatever our staff give.

In 2020, we raised approximately £600,000 for charitable causes (£300,000 directly from staff and a further £300,000 from the Trust). This has proven to be beneficial because it gets people into the habit of philanthropy and once it's a habit it becomes a joy. With our customers, we have built a donor advised fund, which is a master charitable trust. The results have been astonishing! It has way exceeded our expectations because about ten percent of the UK market has given away one hundred million pounds in the last nine years. And we are just beginning!

It has also got a pot of money which is available to any of the three thousand cousins and if they are getting stuck in their own charitable causes, we will contribute. We try to find causes where we can make a sustainable, catalytic, and sometimes systemic difference, and we try to pin them to the United Nations social development goals.

The other good thing is the endowment of the Golden Bottle Trust. We have an endowment so that we can do multi-year commitments. And even if the bank fails it does not affect any one of these multi-year commitments. The Endowment is one hundred percent invested in impact investments. And that is sustainable philanthropy.

Aligned Professional Advisors

Aligned advisers have been fantastically helpful to us. The most useful thing the regulator ever did to us, was to tell us to get some non-executive directors, who have been excellent. One of them urged us to get an executive coach, and that opened the whole world of effective communication.

Our personal family lives are kept separate from the business. If any new cousin wants to be involved in the business, they must share our values and we do psychometric tests to make sure of this.

The best question I have never been asked

During our interview Nicholas raised the best question that many family businesses must answer: *How do you deal with nepotism?*

We are lucky that we now have a pool of more than three thousand cousins to choose from but the best way to deal with nepotism is to use *meritocracy*. It is essential to recognise that the best people to manage a business might not be the best people to own the business. So, we place more emphasis on ownership and stewardship, and we employ good people to do that day-to-day management.

It helps to bring in external people to run the business — even at the CEO level. I was the last family member to be chief executive and I had a very good run.

We had a great crash in 2008 and I realised that I was in a very ambiguous position. You are always conflicted between your management team and your family partners. I just thought, why would you put cousins in that conflict? It is very stressful.

I decided to step down despite having a very good run. This is because I had worked out that all organisations end up shooting their chief executive and I did not want my cousins shooting me! We have seen several family businesses in the past fail because the family CEO refuses to step down or has no succession plan.

The biggest problem faced by wealthy families today is how to get their children to appreciate money, and how to retain their ambition so that they are hungry to achieve. Implementing the *Four Fundamentals* is vital if you wish your family to not just survive but thrive for multiple generations. It starts by reading Nicholas Charles's book, learning from the failings of other families, creating solid governance structures within the family dynamic, and then keeping your family inspired by coming to our bank to help you formulate your own sustainable philanthropic arm.

In any case, it starts by having a deeper understanding and appreciation of the real value of wealth.

NICHOLAS CHARLES & ANTOANETA PROCTOR

18

Preface

Nicholas Charles

*'It has left me with nothing to hope for, with nothing definite
to seek or strive for. Inherited wealth is a real handicap to happiness.
It is as certain death to ambition as cocaine is to morality.'*

William Kissam Vanderbilt

Grandson of the self-made Cornelius Vanderbilt

Just imagine spending all your life building a business and accumulating wealth that should, by right, establish your legacy and family name. Yet, by the time your grandchildren come of age, the wealth you worked so hard to establish, has completely gone. Sadly, this was a problem that my own family suffered. My great-grandfather was a multi-millionaire, yet by the time my father reached the age of eight, the wealth had been completely dissipated. He came to England with nothing to his name and had to restart the wealth-building process from the beginning. As a teenager growing up and listening to this story, I was engulfed by fear and stress that I was destined to follow my ancestors and lose all the wealth my father had built.

I became determined to discover how I could break this seemingly inevitable cycle.

In my first book, entitled *The Four Fundamentals of Family Prosperity*, I uncovered the stories and data that supported the statement that *'more than 90% of wealthy families lose all their wealth within three generations and that 70% will lose it within just two.'*

I discovered that too many families overly rely on their traditional professional advisors to protect their estates.

As a Chartered Certified Accountant and legacy advisor to high-net-worth families, I know that estate planning is not sufficient on its own to secure a family's wealth and legacy.

When I became a qualified accountant and tax advisor, I was very successful in saving my clients millions of pounds in tax. However, I soon realised that despite prudent tax advice this was not sufficient because certain family clients still managed to lose all their wealth. It became evident to me that the underlying problem to family wealth issues was family conflict; and the failure to have an adequate plan to prevent and deal with family conflict. A family breakdown will always lead to a financial meltdown.

I created a solution to deal with these real issues and focused my efforts on educating and empowering families to be able to develop a plan to successfully bring about a financial and human legacy that would be sustainable over multiple generations.

I called this solution *The Four Fundamentals of Family Prosperity.* I designed an illustration to highlight what was required to create a financial legacy that thrives for multiple generations:

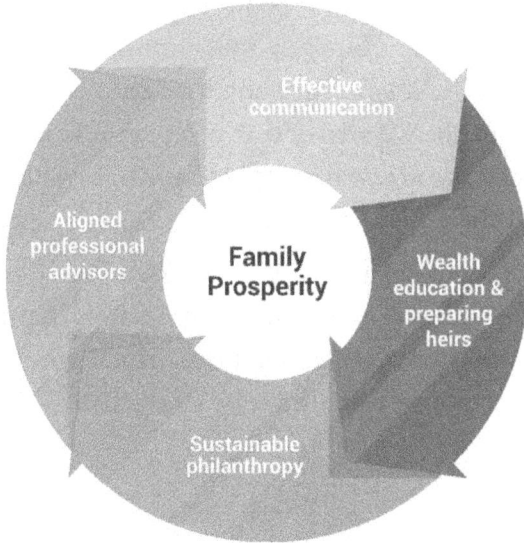

My first book was merely an introduction to family prosperity and provided a foundation for families to work with.

However, it soon became evident that families needed more information.

It was then that I decided to team up with a world-class, private client lawyer, Antoaneta Proctor, who shared my values and passion for helping families. She is also an expert in international tax, evaluating tax risk, cross-border succession, structuring for wealth preservation, and family governance. She attended one of my speaking events, and I soon realised that it was essential that I interview her about family wealth, her experiences, and real-life stories which she had encountered through her client base.

I wanted to expand the message about the importance of this subject.

We originally planned for a forty-five-minute interview, but the conversation was still flowing after one and a half hours. What we spoke about then became the basis for this new book. If my first book can be seen as a starter, then this is the main course!

We wanted to create a book that was informative and interesting but flowed naturally. We did not want to release another dry textbook about family wealth. We advise that you read it from start to finish and highlight all the areas that apply to you and your family so that you can revisit them in the future.

We hope you enjoy reading this book as much as we enjoyed creating it. We wish you and your family a happy, harmonious, and prosperous future for many generations. You are not on your own in this journey, and we can always be contacted to help you if you need us to.

PART 1

What Do We Mean?

The Building Blocks

When we talk about *families*, we mean *wealthy families* with at least GBP£50 million in net assets (and USD$55m). However, all families with an element of wealth can learn from the advice and stories presented in this book. For example, we have witnessed family relationships that have imploded over the gift of just a single property in the UK.

This book explains why this outcome is highly predictable and, sadly, all too common.

fortune

noun

1. chance or luck as an arbitrary force affecting human affairs.

2. c large amount of money or assets.

Family wealth planning

phrase

1. an approach to wealth preservation and family governance.

2. the importance of nurturing character, self-confidence, and respect for the value of people and capital.

3. prudent guidelines for patriarchs, matriarchs, next generations, key intermediaries, trustees, beneficiaries, and trusted advisors.

4. an approach to multi-generational wealth management.

5. an appreciation for the interaction of financial and human assets.

What is wealth?

One of the biggest problems that wealthy families face when trying to secure a multi-generational legacy is the failure to appreciate what wealth actually is. Wealth is more than financial wealth. If one cannot understand the full scope of wealth, then how can one ensure that such wealth thrives for multiple generations?

Financial wealth includes:

- Real estate
- Shares in the family businesses
- Money, including all currencies
- Listed stocks and shares
- Jewellery and valuable commodities, such as gold
- Art
- Intellectual property rights
- Digital assets, such as crypto currencies
- Other

However, is wealth limited to just financial wealth? Unfortunately, most families behave as if that were the case.

When discussing their estates with their advisors and what they wish to gift to the next generation, the conversations are typically restricted to financial wealth alone.

When researching the most successful families, it quickly becomes obvious that the reason why they successfully retained financial wealth for multiple generations is that they ensured that all their wealth was transferred to the next and future generations.

The following are the various forms that wealth include:

- Financial Capital – as we have already explained above, these are the conventional forms of wealth.

- Human Capital – this encompasses the people within your family: their relationships, health, happiness, talents, and potential. This ensures that each person is given the opportunity to pursue their own happiness and fulfilment. There is nothing more important in your family than its people. Nothing will place your financial capital at risk more than human capital that has not been nurtured and developed.

- Intellectual Capital – these are the values, traditions, history, and culture of your family. It is the education, reputation, and life experiences of all your family members. These are the things that give your family its distinctive identity.

- Social Capital - this is the impact you make on society through your efforts, giftings, donations, leadership, and sacrifice. It is an asset that does not show up on your family's own balance sheet, but one you deserve credit for, nonetheless. The development of social capital becomes an outward expression of your family's values and the instrument of your long-term legacy.

If you wish for your family to retain its financial capital for multiple generations, it is essential that the family identifies, captures, and capitalises on these intangible assets and ensures that *all* its' wealth is successfully passed down to the next and future generations.

Family Prosperity, via the Charles Group, and spearheaded by Nicholas Charles, offers a range of client services and strategies that are bespoke to the wants, needs and priorities of each family. These include facilitating family meetings, developing and building on families' purposeful vision, educating the next generation to become 'good beneficiaries', and helping families create a philanthropic arm that inspires each family member to help protect and grow your family's wealth in all its guises.

Inheritance
Proverbs 13:22: A good man leaves an inheritance to his children's children.
The Bible, New King James Version

Even if you are not religious, this biblical verse keeps our life goals, vision, and legacy front and centre when choosing how to use our money today. When we weigh what we want now against what we really want later, one realises how immediate satisfaction needs to be balanced by a focus on the future; and a legacy of purpose and generational fulfilment.

This typically leads to the consideration of lifetime giving, inheritance, and legacy.

Your thoughts:

- *Does your family have a strategy for gifting assets to the next generation?*

- *What legacy has been transmitted to you, and what legacy would you like to transmit?*

- *What values and family stories form or should form part of that legacy?*

Wealthy Family

*'Anybody who thinks money will make you happy,
hasn't got money.'*

David Geffen

Founder of DreamWorks worth $5.5 billion

When someone starts a business, the goal is often to make money to provide a comfortable lifestyle for their family.

When someone makes a lot of money, when they create wealth – build a fortune – of course, the goal is still to benefit their immediate family right now, but invariably the focus also shifts to the future, to the family's ongoing wealth. The focus transfers onto the next generation and more.

This book is essentially a conversation that two trusted advisors – stewards – have about family wealth. More importantly, it is a conversation that wealthy families need to have sooner if they want to manage, preserve and grow their financial and human assets across several generations.

The two go together.

At first reading, it is an introduction to preserving multi-generational family wealth from an accounting and legal perspective. However, its aim is to clarify the broader legacy of family wealth, including the human, intellectual and social aspects of it.

We are looking at family wealth from the perspective of what has been documented over the last 300 years and more. There are exceptions, of course, but typically it appears that the first generation makes the wealth, the second generation manages it, and, regrettably, the third generation loses it. This anomaly has been occurring for hundreds of years, and the amount of money is irrelevant.

Take Cornelius Vanderbilt as a classic example. When he passed away in 1877, he left a collective worth of $143 billion[1] to his family. Unfortunately, he failed to pass down to his children the knowledge of how to retain the wealth for multiple generations. In 1973, when the Vanderbilt family met up, there was not a single millionaire amongst them. The fortune had completely gone.

The common analogy used to describe the acquisition, growth, and loss of family wealth is *shirt sleeves to shirt sleeves in three generations.*

Statistically, the reality is that:

... 70% of family wealth will fall over within two generations. That statistic climbs sharply beyond 90% when the wealth reaches three generations.

We know *what* happens.

Why it happens comes as a surprise to many families.

In fact, one of the major challenges faced by wealthy families today is their inability to understand and appreciate the real causes of multi-generational financial failure. Amazingly, they have very little to do with finance, taxation, estate planning, or wealth planning in general. Yet when one looks at traditional professional advisors today, their attention is directed predominantly on protecting 'the money.' Wealth managers, lawyers, tax advisors, estate planners, accountants, and trustees – the list of such types of advisors is almost limitless.

[1] In 2007 United States Dollars, according to The Wealthy 100 by Michael Klepper and Robert Gunther

However, the management of the money is not the main reason why families fail to retain their wealth for multiple generations. Luckily, consumer protection legislation has developed globally to reduce the risks of negligence and fraud caused by such advisors.

If the management of the money is not the root cause of multi-generational financial failure, then what is?

The most detailed study into this anomaly was conducted by Vic Preisser and Roy Williams from the Williams Group. They studied 3,250 families over a twenty-five-year period to ascertain the true causes of why families failed to retain their wealth for multiple generations. Whilst the results may surprise some readers, on review, it makes perfect sense:

- 60% of families failed because of poor communication and lack of trust amongst family members
- 25% failed because they did not prepare the heirs to receive the wealth
- 10% failed because the family lacked a collective vision for the wealth
- Only 5% failed for other reasons

Whilst the professional industry is geared to help families manage their wealth, who is out there to help families manage their members and empower them to make great decisions about their fortune?

This book builds on a huge body of research into what successful, wealthy families do well.

Naturally, we will also concentrate on the key areas highlighted above, such as establishing open communication, sharing visions and information, heir training, and the need to make this a conscious, deliberate, far-reaching, and sustained focus.

This will then lead to discussions about governance, advisory support, and defensive planning.

Wealth preservation, management, and growth across generations – leaving a legacy – is a very topical and important issue for wealthy families. Nobody wants to work their entire life to build a fortune just so their heirs can self-destruct and lose it all. However, this will be an inevitable reality if the ideas and concepts described in this book are not actioned.

Unfortunately, most families struggle to bring the issue of succession to the surface - as something to be discussed today and not 'sometime in the future', and certainly not after somebody is demised. These conversations may not be easy to have and may cause emotional upheaval and even friction within the family, but the risks of not having them are too great to ignore.

Nobody has ever created a successful business by following a strategy of luck and hope for the future. So why follow such a strategy for your family? Great businesses are built on the back of a vision that all involved within the business are inspired to follow, regular communication amongst the key stakeholders, and solid governance structures and strategies to take on opportunities and deal with threats.

From our perspective, the biggest shortcoming that wealthy families face is that they do not anticipate or deal with the likely challenges of succession today; they leave these important issues until tomorrow. This tendency is called normality bias – the false assumption that just because things are going well today, they will always go well in the future. Failing to have a plan is planning to fail, and this always comes with a far-reaching financial, relational and emotional price tag. Families rarely demonstrate appreciation that the best time to implement family prosperity strategies is when the family has no obvious signs of disharmony or irreversible conflicts.

All families argue from time to time, and no families are perfect because they are all represented by imperfect human beings. However, successful families have processes and systems in place to ensure that disagreements are discussed openly and managed with tact and wisdom before they escalate into all-out warfare!

Arguments usually come about when families do not have a strategy for communicating decisions around gifting and succession to roles to the next generation.

The biggest mistake many families make is to wait and simply allow a parent's Will to communicate to the heirs who is going to receive what. The problem with this is that Wills do not provide two-way communication; the donor has passed away, leaving uncertainty amongst the beneficiaries as to why certain gifts were made and stoking fears that siblings were better loved. Such uncertainties can result in emotional conflict, causing the implosion of family relations and leading to damaging litigation and even death.

Case Study: The Chadha Brothers

When Kulwant Chadha passed away, he did not leave much clarity regarding how significant family business and personal assets were to pass to the next generation. This created huge tension between his two sons, Ponty and Hardeep Chadha, who met in November 2012 at one of their family farmhouses in Chhatarpur, Delhi, to argue over their inheritance and the settlement had been brokered by their mother. Accompanied by their bodyguards, this argument escalated into a fierce gun battle in which both brothers were shot and killed.

For a family reported to have assets worth more than US$10 billion, it would be hard to imagine that Ponty and Hardeep's father could have ever dreamed that his sons would die in a gun battle over their inheritance.

PART 2

Communication

Are We Really Talking? If Not, Why Not?

Wealthy families appreciate legacy planning. Nobody wants to see all their hard work destroyed within one or two generations. However, in recent times this term has been confused with estate planning. Whilst they may appear similar there are important and significant differences. Estate planning is simply arranging your estate in the most tax efficient manner and focuses solely on financial capital. Most families tend to be very good at dealing with their estate planning through their team of tax and legal advisors.

Legacy planning involves establishing the foundations, principles, purposeful vision and communication structures to ensure that all forms of the family's wealth is retained for multiple generations. Unfortunately, many families fail to appreciate this important difference between estate planning and legacy planning. If you want to establish a legacy that thrives for multiple generations then take action now.

Quite simply if you want your wealth to thrive for multiple generations then you must understand and implement the concept of the business of being a family. The difficulty with this is that there are emotional connotations to treating a family like a business. After all you cannot sack your family member for being incompetent! Every family is different and as such there is no such thing as 'one size fits all'.

Every solution will be unique in accordance with the make-up and requirements of each family. This can range from setting up formal communication structures, right through to the creation of complex governance structures based around a family constitution that all family members are inspired to follow. It is essential to start to implement some form of governance structure around the family dynamic.

Sadly, when it comes to looking after the family's human capital, in the sense of communicating with and bringing up the next generation of leaders, we find that these conversations are either not taking place at all or being delayed for too long. We have even found that parents fail to discuss what their expectations are for the next generation of family members.

Often, it is difficult to create a forum or an outlet for such discussions. Ideally, it should be the independent trusted advisors/mediators around the family who should bring out those conversations and put them onto the table where the family is not already engaging in them. In seeking to facilitate open communication around what are often emotional topics, trusted advisers need to identify not only what families want but also what they need to achieve their objectives for preserving and stewarding the family's capital, both financial and human.

Our concern is that most families preoccupy themselves purely with the financial wealth and transfer just the financial wealth to the next generation, as opposed to the total wealth, including their human and intellectual capital. Our challenge is: how do we, as advisers, help families ensure that the total wealth is transferred to the next generation? And how do we help them establish a culture of communicating regularly with the next generation, from a young age, on succession and business continuity topics so that they develop an age-appropriate understanding of and appreciation for the family's wealth?

As professional advisors, we see families, or the senior generation, coming to discuss creating tax-efficient structures or wills, which deal with the transfer of the financial assets. We try to broaden the conversation by encouraging families to consider the human context within which the family structure(s) will need to operate.

Every family has an operating system: spoken or unspoken rules on how they operate. It is fundamental for this operating system to be understood, brought to a conscious level, gently and constructively challenged if necessary, and most importantly, it (or a modified version of it) accepted by all the family members if it is to act as the blueprint for how the family governs itself. This requires the current generation to be open to bringing in a wider circle of the family members, who are not only invited to sit around the table in an observer capacity but have a voice that allows them to participate in the shaping of the family's governance framework.

But families tend to struggle with the notion of wider participation.

As an example, Antoaneta was working with a substantially wealthy family who approached her for inheritance tax advice. She wrote an excellent report, twenty-five-pages long, and amongst those twenty-five pages, there was one sentence that advised, 'you should consider putting in place a family constitution.'

A *family constitution* is a written document that aims to create a guiding protocol with regards to the governance of the family as a whole. It establishes a set of rules and in turn details the family's core values, vision, mission and governance structure for navigating the family's affairs. The advantage of a family constitution is that it ensures clarity, transparency and families know what to do when disagreements arise. It addition it strengthens the family's emotional cohesion because all the individual family members work together to formulate the constitution.

Antoaneta spent the next seven months working with that family, helping them to create a family constitution. An important part of the work she did with the family was that she raised the question early on as to how her clients envisaged engaging the next generation in those discussions.

Antoaneta's recommendation was that she has one-to-one conversations with each family member (both parents and children), asking them to each complete separate questionnaires and then comparing their responses. The purpose would be two-fold. Firstly, to bring out on a conscious level any differences of views, expectations and concerns – between the generations, but also between members of the same generation - and provide a forum for them to be discussed openly, without judgment. Secondly, and just as importantly, doing so would allow the family to identify where there is a commonality in thinking, the areas of overlap, and the shared values that define the family and make them who they are.

Even though the family was very enthusiastic about implementing a family constitution, the parents thought that the first step should be to effectively elicit their own vision of what the family constitution should look like and only then bring in the next generation. So, they were willing to have their children sit around the discussion table, but only after they had crystallised their own thinking.

That approach allowed for a managed discussion. There is a clear path ... which the senior generation has charted beforehand. In effect, however, younger family members have limited input; they get to play around the fringes but not necessarily influence the fundamental framework.

The lack of meaningful participation by the next generation in governance discussions is a key issue for families to address if they are to create family constitutions that endure beyond the current generation and are not merely relegated to a dusty drawer.

Whether you decide to start with a blank slate and formulate your family's constitution (governance rulebook), with all the family members involved from the outset or prefer to create the outline and then present it to your family, one thing is very clear. It is essential that you start the process now! Creating a family constitution is not easy but it will establish the foundations to retain and grow your family's wealth for multiple generations.

Can your family afford the risk to delay the creation and implementation of a family constitution?

Creating a safe environment that encourages the family to discuss openly what is important to its individual members and establish a shared legacy is crucial to ensuring that your family thrives for multiple generations. This does not necessarily, or even mainly, mean discussing the "dry" and "confusing" subjects of tax, wealth structures, wills, etc. Family discussions need to be engaging, meaningful and even fun to capture the attention of all generations and lay the foundations for creating a shared family legacy. Holding such discussions will also begin the process of creating roles and defining responsibilities within the family, which leads to effective family governance. The larger your family and the more substantial the wealth that you must look after, the greater the importance of formulating governance structures that have the buy-in of current, next and future generations; but it all begins with setting aside the time, at least once a quarter, to hold family meetings for the family to come together and share its vision for the future through open communication.

Your thoughts:

- *Does your family hold regular meetings at which broader issues beyond the family business or investment strategy are discussed?*

- *If not, what do you think needs to happen for the channels of communication to be opened on a family-wide basis?*

- *If you are, do you feel that these meetings offer the opportunity for meaningful engagement for all the family members?*

- *What does meaningful engagement mean to you?*

Do We Need A Family Constitution?

What is a *family constitution?*

Put very simply, the family constitution (also referred to as a family charter) is the rulebook on how the family governs itself, interacts with each other and operates as a family.

It typically includes your family's story - how it all started, what made your family who they are, what challenges they faced and important lessons they learned through those experiences, as well as philosophies, values, principles and vision for the future to guide future generations. The family constitution also sets out the family members' roles and responsibilities, and processes for self-governance, including how assets will be protected, succession handled, the leadership of family businesses selected, and family disputes resolved.

Alongside the family constitution, families would typically create a mission statement that sets out the purpose and vision for the family. Why you are trying to preserve, protect and perpetuate the family's wealth.

What you include in these documents will serve as signposts for future generations.

Since Family Constitutions are not binding, why have one?

Families that need to be persuaded of the value of family constitutions often question their utility on the basis that they are not binding. And they are right to point this out.

However, to answer their question with a question, even if the family ends up never signing a document, would there be value in a process that involves family members – from different generations, blended families, multi-jurisdictional, multi-cultural - sitting around the table and communicating with each other openly and working together towards a common goal, maybe for the first time in years?

Such a process, which opens the channels of communication between the family members and builds that little bit more trust between them, is invaluable both for the family and for its advisors.

Moreover, although not a legally binding document itself, many of the provisions of a family constitution will percolate and be hard-wired into related documents, such as trust deeds, shareholders' agreements, co-ownership agreements, nuptial agreements and other governance arrangements which will be legally binding[1]. The family constitution is the overarching framework, underneath which sit various structuring solutions and legal documents, all of which need to work in tandem and which together give legal certainty to the family.

What if a family member or branch of the family is unwilling to engage with or refuses to abide by the family constitution?

Apart from the simple case of a 'rogue' family member, this is most likely to happen in one of three types of situations:

1. If that family member or branch has not been sufficiently

---

[1] In the case of nuptial agreements, depending on the governing law and where any divorce proceedings may take place

and meaningfully involved in the shaping of the family constitution and therefore feels that what ought to be a unified vision for the family does not actually represent them, i.e., they feel disenfranchised.

2. Where there is a history of family disagreement, resulting in loss of trust. Despite family members often being able to patch up their differences and reach a *modus operandi*[2] they can all live with, there often remains an undercurrent of mistrust, which stands in the way of the family members' listening to each other. Being able to dissolve tensions through a fair process, which results in a fair outcome for all concerned, can pave the way for family harmony to be restored. However, the impetus to create dispute-resolution processes, typically as part of the family constitution, can come too late for some families.

A client of Antoaneta's once shared with her that their family (being the fourth generation of wealth) was in the process of crafting a family constitution; however, with version five of the document under discussion, there seemed to be no end in sight for this process to complete to the satisfaction of all involved. This was causing a great deal of frustration and disillusionment with what the family constitution and consensus-building process could deliver. To the experienced, outside adviser with knowledge of the family's history and dynamics, it was clear that past family disagreements were continuing to play out in the family discussion forum.

3. Where families are locked together in a common enterprise by virtue of being shareholders in successful family businesses but lack a common purpose as a family. The business continues to operate through the

---

[2] Latin for a mode of operation.

professionalisation of management so long as the disparate family members continue to receive their usual income streams. However, challenges are likely to emerge where the strategic direction for the business means that current income needs to be sacrificed for future growth and returns.

*'There are two things that can destroy a family business:
the business and the family, and they both have to be kept in order.'*

Alexander Hoare

C Hoare and Co Private Bank

Where the desire is to build, through the creation of a family constitution, something bigger than the sum of the family's individual parts and not limited to the role of family members as shareholders, careful consideration should be given to how 'the family' is defined. Pruning the family tree is a necessary component of keeping it healthy and preserving its vitality. Moreover, family members need to be free to follow their own chosen paths whilst always having the option of remaining within the family and participating in (some of) its structures. It is essential that the family regularly meets up to communicate the fact that each family member will be supported and allowed to follow their own chosen path to happiness. You do not want members of your family to feel forced to working for the family business because they fear being ostracised from the family itself.

Is the family constitution an expression of the parents' vision for future generations?

There is a misconception that family governance is all about the founding generation's wishes, values, and vision.

This can be the result of confusing 'governance' with the structuring tools that families use to plan for succession, such as trusts, foundations, family investment companies, family partnerships, etc. However, structures (such as trusts and offshore holding companies) are mainly about preservation and stewarding of the family's financial wealth and less about an overarching governance model that permeates every aspect of how the family is, interacts with each other and governs itself. While the governing documents for family structures, such as the Deed of Trust and associated Letters of Wishes, would be precisely that – an expression of the settlor's wishes for how the structure should be administered – a family constitution relies for its legitimacy on buy-in from the wider family.

And the differences go further than that.

Unlike structuring, which senior generations can put in place and not even tell their children about for years (for fear of breeding a dependency culture), a family cannot have a formal governance framework and not know about it. It is precisely that knowledge - of what the family defines as acceptable behaviour, worthwhile contribution, and family legacy - that provides the antidote to many potentially destructive sides of wealth and, even more so, extreme wealth.

Having said that, both the family office and structuring aspects can be used as a springboard to facilitate governance conversations and as the means through which governance is delivered and embedded. For example, trust structures administered by Private Trust Companies (PTCs) or advised by investment committees will invariably require consideration of the composition such PTC boards and committees; the nomination, election, and voting rights of board and committee members to ensure that no branch of the family is disenfranchised, while at the same time making sure that the best person for the job gets appointed to the role, and so forth.

Similarly, where the family office has a role that goes beyond investment management, it can be instrumental in consensus-building, value-setting, and the transmission of a family's culture across multiple generations, all of which are components of effective family governance.

Ultimately, family governance is the umbrella underneath which all other components, such as the family office, structuring, next generation education, family communication, etc., sit. As such, it is all-encompassing. It cannot be measured against the yardstick of a single individual's wishes or vision, and where it seemingly is, it will never endure beyond the lifetime of that individual.

The family constitution needs to be a living, breathing 'thing' that family members buy into, not something that can be imposed on them (at least not in the long term).

But still, the impetus for the creation of a family constitution invariably comes from the senior generation, does it not?

It can and often does. But it does not necessarily have to.

There is another common misconception – that family governance is all about what happens when the current generation is no longer there; that it is essentially about succession and post-death planning. It is thus little wonder that next generation family members would shy away from asking the important questions, lest they be seen as wishing their parents gone.

But there are so many more questions that families should be discussing!

Children need to be asking what their parents' expectations of them are. If there is a family business, is it the expectation that children should join at entry-level and work their way up the corporate leadership structure? Or are they expected to gain specialist experience externally first before joining the family business?

What happens if they wish to pursue their own independent path in life altogether? What is the aspiration for the family as a whole, and what does success look like where children's personalities, interests, and skill sets are very different?

Much the same questions ought to be exercising the thinking of the current generation. They also need to be asking themselves if their children have been equipped with what they need to be fulfilled and successful. Have they done what it takes to prepare the next generation of leaders? Have they questioned their own assumptions? Have they verified them with the people they expect to continue the family legacy, whether in relation to family businesses, philanthropy, or generally?

This also raises the question of when the optimum time is to involve the next generation in the management of wealth and to get their buy-in for both the structures set up by their parents and the governance model adopted by the whole family.

There is a clear tension between access to information and transparency on the one hand and the control of information and assets by the senior generations. This is a fundamental dynamic in cross-generational planning. How it is resolved often depends on what the senior generation is willing to do and when, but there are essentially three questions packed into one, namely, at what ages or stage will next generation family members be provided with each of:

- access to information;
- participation in the family's decision-making processes; and
- control over any portion of their 'inheritance.'

As professional trusted advisers, we take the view that the question of timing is less about divulging the full balance sheet and more about gradually introducing the next and future generations to the family business, if there is one; types of investments and structures the family has and teaching them how to be 'responsible citizens' within the context of these. All too often, children are 'taught' not to talk about money (typically for fear of them becoming entitled), with many having no clue about the value of money or how to handle it. This leaves successor generations unprepared for the responsibility of stewarding wealth. The result is often what their parents feared the most – the dissipation of such wealth.

The best-prepared families deliberately go about creating opportunities for discussion, constructive challenge, learning, and decision-making, often starting at a young age. We encourage our clients to help facilitate great discussions by organising an annual retreat. This facilitates an ideal platform for teaching and sharing information with the next generation. It also provides a great escape from the usual stresses of daily life and can be a great way to solidify the relationships amongst the individual family members.

In our experience, the successful families introduce the next generation to managing wealth on a gradual, consistent, step by step process. The next generation are given the opportunity to oversee a small fund first, in relation to which they may take the lead (with the right level of support) on the asset allocation, risk and return parameters, etc. with them reporting back to the family. This is not just an opportunity to learn financial skills but also about working collaboratively.

Where there are family businesses involved, apart from getting to know the nuts and bolts of those from a young age, there may be the opportunity to join board deliberations as an observer first. Having formal guidelines and a process for family members who wish to work in the business, laying down minimum educational and work qualifications (often involving work experience outside the family business), and an objective application process is also essential.

The better developed the channels of communication and the more regularly the communication muscle is used by the family, the easier it is for next generation family members to broach governance topics (amongst any other) with their elders and peers.

Does a family constitution necessarily avoid family disputes?

As successive generations become further removed from the founder generation who accumulated the initial wealth, a sense of entitlement and lack of familial ties could threaten the success of generational wealth transfers, and disputes become more likely, especially at times of economic or family stresses.

Fostering consensus and coherent family vision among family members who may have different expectations for the allocation of the family's assets may become less easy to achieve. Failure to develop an alignment of goals across generations can lead to fracture and disunity.

Leadership that encourages transparency within the family and buy-in of a shared philosophy across the generations can help overcome these pitfalls.

A family governance framework needs to do two things:

1. aid the prevention of family disputes; and
2. provide a mechanism for managing and resolving them.

Prevention is best achieved through family members building a sense of connection, both to each other and more broadly to the family as an 'institution.'

Therefore, it is key to tell the family's story and transmit the family's core values to successive generations. Unfortunately, most families have not shared their family's story with their children, let alone with future generations. Expecting that they will pick those values up by osmosis is not always realistic. And it is much more difficult to build those connections in what can be the emotionally charged circumstances at the point of succession or when a dispute is already brewing.

Open and regular communication is a key element in building cohesion and connection among family members. Family retreats can provide a platform for family members to create alignment, report on progress, educate next and future generations, and make important decisions that affect the whole family.

A family constitution provides a framework for all of this to happen, as well as typically incorporating mechanisms for the management and resolution of family disputes, often through the involvement of elders.

Your thoughts:

Has your family got, or begun the process of creating a family constitution?

If you have a family constitution in place already:

- *Were you involved in its shaping, and do you feel that it captures the hopes, concerns, and aspirations of all the family?*
- *Does your family live by it? Is it guided regularly by what the family constitution provides, or is it just another document that the family rarely, if ever, looks it?*
- *Do you know what it provides in the event of different eventualities? Have you been educated on the scope and terms of the family constitution?*

If your family has not implemented a family constitution yet:

- *Do you see value in the family having one? If so, what?*
- *What conversations need to happen, and who needs to be involved in them to build momentum for this process to happen?*
- *What role can you personally play in it?*

Communication Is THE Key
To Multi-Generational Wealth

So, your family has implemented a family constitution. What happens next?

When we meet with families, we emphasise just how important communication is within the family dynamic. Communication is the foundation for everything else; it needs to be built upon.

We touched upon some families' wanting to create a vision for themselves and their wealth but being reluctant to incorporate the next generation as part of those discussions when they are still working from a tabula rasa[1].

But this is the point at which you are shaping the future and the governance framework within which you see that vision unfolding. If you want it to be a shared vision, therefore, then the sooner you engage the next generation in those conversations, the better. Because the risk of your family not doing so is that when you get to the transition from one generation to the next – usually on the passing of a senior family member - the next generation would look at the constitution and think, *'Well, it does not embody my vision for the future* and scrap it.

---

[1] Latin for scraped tablet, i.e., a clean slate

Even worse, the constitution could end up becoming just another document that is gathering dust in some cupboard, sitting in somebody's office, never consulted, and mostly forgotten about. A formal constitution needs to capture what you stand for as a family. It is not some sort of document that nobody ever looks at but that miraculously creates healthy family relations and cohesion. It should be the embodiment of how the family operates and how it relates to each other and the outside world. Otherwise, it is irrelevant and of no consequence.

The constitution or aspects of it should be discussed by the family regularly - at retreats or otherwise - to ensure there is a common understanding of its key provisions and awareness by the family members of their rights and responsibilities as such. It is part of educating the next generation and continuing to mould and reinforce the family consensus.

The constitution should be reviewed by the family regularly. Not too often, as its role is to create continuity and provide enduring guidance for generations to come. Revising it at least once every five years and on the happening of key events for the family should ensure that it evolves with the family and continues to encompass what it stands for and believes in.

A family constitution that is enforced upon the family members is like having a mission or vision statement for a company that none of the stakeholders buy into. It is just a fancy set of words on a piece of paper or a website, which is pointless! The most powerful and the most successful companies are the ones where you see that all the stakeholders - the employees, the shareholders, the directors - all buy into that common vision.

A family vision statement needs to inspire the entire family. The family constitution needs buy-in from all family members, and communication and participation are what ensure this. It is essential that all family members are part of the conversation and involved in the creation and subsequent review of these documents as they forge a path that the family is inspired to follow.

As time passes by, life occasionally starts getting in the way, and whilst the family is important, individual family members need to be free to follow their own pursuit of happiness. In some cases, this will best be realised within the constructs of the family business, philanthropic projects sponsored or spearheaded by the family, or within the family office. But sometimes, it may take family members in different directions outside the family structures. In either case, family members should feel able to articulate their personal viewpoints and be supported in their choices - to remain within or opt-out of the family's collective enterprises, and this should never be treated as a one-way street (i.e., once out, always out). The more flexibility there is, the more likely the family is to preserve its unity and harmony. Family members need to be allowed to choose what the pursuit of happiness means to them personally, to opt into the family's structures as a whole or specific family project on a case-by-case basis, or to fluidly move between external roles and being part of the family business. It is the family constitution that defines the family's approach to these issues; by de-personalising them, it takes the emotional charge out of discussions about them.

Therefore, when you meet up as a family and are debating how you wish to respond to challenges that the family is facing, you would typically go back to the constitution, specifically paying attention to the family's stated purpose and vision and use that as a springboard to facilitate sound decision-making through effective communication.

So why do families struggle to have these conversations?

Essentially, because they are perceived as, and indeed can be, too emotional. Without an objective criterion that applies across the

NICHOLAS CHARLES & ANTOANETA PROCTOR

board to all family members, a well-meaning conversation started by the next generation and aimed at getting clarity about family expectations from them can be misinterpreted as impatience, lack of respect and even rapaciousness. Likewise, senior generations who are guided by what they believe is best for their children may often be surprised at how different the next generation's own perceptions are of what would make them fulfilled.

Where open, two-way communication is not the norm within the family, initiating such conversations can risk an argument and most families prefer to avoid confrontation – even though ignoring such discussions is detrimental to establishing and preserving your family's harmony and legacy.

Your thoughts:

- *On a scale of one to ten - one being non-existent and ten being regular structured conversations - how often does your family meet up to communicate the family's vision, discuss challenges collectively and provide an update on the "state of the family," including the family business, assets, gifting strategy and aspirations for the future?*

- *What sort of issues would you like to see discussed by your family in an open forum that are not currently being considered?*

- *What would the opportunity of having such discussions mean to you?*

- *How can you convey the importance of such conversations happening within the family?*

- *Who can help you to create an opening for such conversations to take place?*

Emotions And Wealth

Individuals can deal with rational arguments about finances, investments and structures for the holding of wealth. But when it comes to including the next generation in those discussions, this tends to trigger a lot of emotional charges.

In some respects, this is unsurprising.

Senior generations would like to see their children forge their own way in life, developing into successful and fulfilled individuals, and steer them away from the trappings of wealth and entitled living. This is hugely important to any parent. But avoiding talking about wealth does little to achieve this.

With children attending prestigious schools alongside other young people from evidently privileged backgrounds; going on luxury holidays and the one-upmanship of sharing pictures on social media with their peers as evidence of these experiences, it does not exactly require a stretch of the imagination for children to know that they are not exactly under-privileged. This is before they stumble upon the family's online footprint and net wealth worth commentary from the likes of Forbes.

Instead, where wealth is not talked about, this creates the preconditions for misconceptions to arise – as to the extent of the family's wealth, its purpose (to be stewarded or enjoyed and the right combination between the two), the intended role of individual family members within family structures and businesses, the relative importance of different contributions to the family, the list is endless. The same is even more true in the context of family businesses.

Culture is clearly a major factor in the context of how families communicate with each other, as it shapes family expectations and values, often linked to religious values. However, it is important to recognise that we live in a smaller world - the next generation of family members are being educated at top universities across the globe, and they are exposed to technology and media in an unprecedented way (often seen as eroding some of the traditional cultural values of the family) - which leads to different expectations, generationally and between members of the same generation depending on their own experiences. This can be difficult emotionally and unsettling to the established family consensus. Understanding how much of those cultural norms go to the core of who the family is and building that sense of shared identity is vital.

For example, assumptions regarding roles and expectations for sons versus daughters can be a challenging mindset to change and can vary widely across cultures. Where the traditional family model is not open to being re-defined, female family members, often Western-educated and just as well qualified as their male siblings, may be left with no option but to realise themselves outside of the family's structures.

Likewise, family-controlled businesses that have 'always' had a family member as CEO can face difficult succession issues where there is no suitable family candidate, particularly where a family member has an expectation of assuming that role. Conversely, a family member can feel an obligation, because of those same assumptions and expectations, to assume a role for which they are not suited and that would be better filled by an outside executive.

These are not exceptional situations, and they are emotionally charged. But unless the family can deal with the challenge in a way that dissolves resentments that are building up and provides an alternative path that restores harmony, family dispute becomes inevitable. One only needs to look at the number of family businesses that have been wrecked by disputes regarding the family members' inheritance and role in leadership.

Think of the Ambani brothers in India. Many of our Indian clients keep referring to this regrettable case of sibling rivalry. The first thing they would say to us when they walk through the door is, *We don't want to be the next Ambani brothers!*

Case Study: The Ambani Brothers

In 2002, when the self-made billionaire, Dhirubhai Ambani, passed away, he left his fortune and conglomerate business empire, Reliance Group, to his two sons – Mukesh and Anil. Unfortunately, his passing created disarray for the family, which saw the two brothers competing against each other for control over the family business. Mukesh used his authority as Chairman to exert his influence over Anil, and this created a conflict that was to last for over a decade. The brothers ended up in a business "divorce," which saw the company split and divided amongst them. However, this did not signal the end of their conflict. In 2009 Anil took his brother's gas company to court, demanding his company be charged for gas at a heavily reduced rate. The brothers stopped talking to each other, and the feud became very bitter. Anil lost the court battle and began to witness his business empire crumble. In 2018 Anil defaulted on his $80 million loans to Ericsson and had to be bailed out by his brother to stop him from going to jail. In 2020, Anil, who at his peak was worth an estimated $42 billion, had to admit in an English court that his net worth was zero!

Although Mukesh may be the richest man in India, the competition with his brother ripped the family apart, divided the company his father had built, and left Anil, his only sibling, bankrupt. One can only wonder if this was the legacy that their father, Dhirubhai, had wanted to leave?

That is what happens when families do not plan or communicate their wishes, aspirations, and intentions for the future. It is a missed opportunity to head off conflict before it has arisen and to deal with emerging pressure lines that have the capacity to develop into full-blown and very destructive conflict. A family prosperity plan encourages family members to deal with emotional issues instead of brushing them under the carpet and allowing them to fester.

No family plans to fail; they simply fail to plan.

But the fact that conversations around business, succession, and contingency planning can be emotional is a major barrier.

In most cases, an objective observer can predict the potential for what are emotional issues today to become disputes in the future. The strife that families endure due to a lack of planning and communication is nowhere more profound and destructive than after the senior generation's demise.

In hindsight, those emotionally charged disputes could have been mitigated or avoided by flushing them out and nipping them in the bud, by preparing for them sooner rather than later.

In dealing with highly emotive issues – often involving the disruption of deeply rooted hierarchical models – it is important that families keep the why at the forefront of their thinking. Why are they doing this? What is the purpose of the family's wealth and of putting in place a family governance framework? If it is to keep the family together, then having the courage to engage in what can be difficult family conversations, emotional intelligence to make those discussions constructive, and the flexibility to embrace change while staying true to one's core values must be key.

Your thoughts:

- *Are you worried about the emotional aspect of having an open conversation with your family about the family's wealth?*

- *If so, do you think that avoiding having such conversations is in the best interests of your family?*

- *What opportunities are there for you to initiate such conversations?*

- *Are there elders in the family who may act as wise and impartial counsel to discuss your concerns with and then help introduce them to the wider family in a non-contentious way?*

- *Are there trusted advisers in-house (within the family office) or who you deal with externally, who have the depth of understanding of the family dynamics and can facilitate a constructive dialogue that builds consensus within, rather than divides.*

How Do We Start The Conversation?

There is a generational aspect to it as well.

Oftentimes the second and subsequent generations will be desperate to discuss governance, mutual expectations, business continuity and their role within it, gifting and inheritance, and so forth with their seniors. But they worry - How do I broach the topic with my parents without appearing disrespectful?

These subjects are often referred to as the 'elephant in the room' because people appreciate the problem but are too afraid to deal with it.

Part of the difficulty can be traced back to the misconception we identified earlier, that when discussing governance, you are talking about a death - what happens after key people are no longer amongst us. Death simply creates a void, emotionally and in terms of a power vacuum where it is unexpected and unplanned for. The solution for dealing with it is effective planning, governance structures, and a legacy that the family continues to treasure and contribute to.

Effective governance begins with the next generation asking broad questions and listening from a position of nothingness (i.e., without preconceived ideas, without making statements that mean anything other than what they say, without letting assumptions fill the spaces between the lines), including the following:

- What are your expectations of me?

- What are the roles and responsibilities of each family member?

- What is required for family members to be involved in the family business?

- Who, if anybody, has been assigned to become the next leader of the family business?

- What does it mean for each family member if they decide to follow a different career outside of the family business?

- What is the exit strategy for the family business?

- How do we, as a family, determine our investment priorities?

- What is our approach to philanthropy and how can I get involved?

- How can I get educated about the family structures, what they are intended to achieve and how they could support the family members in achieving their aspirations?

- What do I need to know and do to be in a position to contribute effectively to the fulfilment of the family's vision?

- Does the family have a family bank, and if so, how can it support a family member?

- What is the current gifting strategy for the family?

- Who are the family's professional advisory team, and which family members are responsible for communicating with them?

It is a matter of two-way communication and education. Not just the seniors educating the next generation about finance, trust structuring, asset protection, estate planning, or other concepts that the young generation will eventually have to deal with, but also about the next generation communicating with their seniors as to how they see themselves fitting in within the family businesses and structures or outside of those.

There is sometimes the challenge of a senior generation where they have made all the decisions in their businesses, calling all the shots, and where they have been very successful at doing that. This generation will struggle to let go of control and power (because no one can do it the way I can and the next generation is simply not ready), but it is essential that they learn to trust and empower the next generation; otherwise, their heirs will be left unprepared, and their family legacy will not have a hope of succeeding. Such family leaders need to find a way of not only imparting their wisdom to the next generation but also mastering the skill of being able to step back and listen to the next generation; likewise, the next generation needs to maintain their respect and reciprocate.

That sort of two-way dialogue does not necessarily come naturally.

Your thoughts:

- *In your family, do you have two-way discussions about family wealth and the family business? If yes, what makes this possible?*
- *If not, why not? What can you do to begin changing this?*

Grown-Ups And Growing Up

If you are the parent of grown-up children, for you, a child is never fully grown up. They are always your child, and you are supposed to guide them and tell them what a rewarding and successful life should look like and what is best for them.

In trying to facilitate governance conversations, we often find the need to coach the senior generation on how to approach the engagement with their children on a peer-to-peer level.

As hard as it might seem, it is about understanding what the next generation wants, including:

- Do they want to, one day, take on the roles and responsibilities of leading the family business or any particular division?

- How do they perceive the interaction between their own aspirations and those of their siblings?

- What do they believe about what it takes to be successful in business and what they can bring to the table?

- What do they see as their own path of happiness, and how do they envisage the family helping and supporting them with it? Do they want to follow a completely different profession?

- How does 'fair' look from their perspective in terms of future gifting, allocation of roles in relation to family structures, and succession planning?

- Do they want to support sustainable philanthropy?

- What do they find difficult in terms of conversations they wish were taking place, involvement in the various aspects of what the family does, next generation education and participation, and how can the family help overcome such challenges in their view?

Children who have benefited from the wealth created by a family business may be expected to step into that family business to ensure that wealth is ongoing and continues to be enhanced. But maybe they do not identify with that business or want to be in business. Maybe they want to be lawyers, actors, or sports persons; maybe they have no intention of running a business, and therefore, based on what they want, they might not be the best person to take over the family business. Yet they may feel pressurised by what they believe the family's expectations to be.

If you are the senior generation and currently running the family business and in charge of the family's wealth, surely, the best time to find out what the next generation wants is during your lifetime. Even if there is a genuine desire by the next generation to take over the family business, the process of learning the ropes of that business, gaining the necessary skills, and becoming an effective leader usually takes five to ten years!

It is essential that this process of self-discovery, learning, and personal growth is put in motion as soon as possible.

You need to bring up the next generation of business leaders, and that takes time. It also requires a fair level of support to take on the challenges ahead.

Never make the mistake of assuming that you know what the next generation wants or does not want to do, whether in terms of taking over the family business or generally. This can lead to family rifts down the line, or a lifetime of unhappiness for dutiful children who truly wished to fulfil their parents' wishes and, in the process, sacrificed their own.

Similarly, business families do not always stay in business or in the same line of business. While business families tend to be serial entrepreneurs and never too far from investing in another great idea, if there is an exit strategy in mind, it is important that this is discussed openly with the next generation. It is a process of communicating the exit strategy to them and with them. Having the opportunity to contribute to the decision-making process, rather than be faced with an irreversible act, ensures that the type of exit agreed upon reflects the family members' own aspirations and no resentments are built up. For example, a partial exit may be agreed upon whereby the family members' participation in the business is reduced but not extinguished if there is the appetite by at least some of the family members to remain involved with it while allowing for diversification to take place. Once a decision has been collectively made, it must be followed through, even if it means selling the business outright and investing or allocating the funds to support the next generation's professional and personal goals.

So, the earlier these conversations start taking place, the better.

Case Study: A Vision for the Whole Family

The parents (a second generation of wealth) of a very substantial family that Antoaneta worked with were asked, *What is your aspiration for the family for the next twenty, fifty, and one hundred years?*

The father simply turned around and, with an element of confidence, said, 'Well, I would expect it to double, triple and quadruple the family's wealth!'

The mother looked rather surprised at that, 'Hang on a second! You've got three very different children. One has entered the property world; another runs the family office, and a third one is a socialite who doesn't know what she wants to do. So how does this vision of success work vis-a-vis the family members?'

It was then that the penny dropped for the father! He had assumed what the family's future would look like *without* consulting with his children or creating a clear vision that involved and inspired his whole family.

If you define success in purely financial terms and by reference to the success of the family business, then anyone who does not take over the family business or remain involved with it is, by that definition, considered a failure.

The parents were so engrossed in what they were good at and loved doing that they had inadvertently ignored, when formulating their definition of success, the question of what their children might need to feel happy. This is understandable for the founders of family businesses, whose life is the business. But children may feel very differently. And it is at that stage that the business of being a family must replace the idea of simply being a family business.

There is a saying that one cannot see the forest for the trees and this analogy aptly describes many families. It is essential that one takes a step back to see the bigger picture, from the perspective of the different family members and not just one's own, and plan accordingly.

With this particular family business, the parents, being the people who created, built and have grown the wealth vehicle, needed to step back and think, "Okay, this is our life. But what is going to be the life of each one of our three very different children, and how can we support them?"

Once they had been able to separate their own perspective from that of their children, the parents were quick to realise that what mattered to them the most was that their children developed great working ethics to be applied in the pursuit of what each of their children felt passionate about. Exactly how hard is it for the next generation to feel a success, and that they are living both their own and their parents' dream on such a definition?

Your thoughts:

- *How well do you know the wishes, aspirations, motivations, and desires of your children?*

- *Is this something you have discussed (and continue to discuss on an ongoing basis) with your children, or are you second-guessing them?*

- *Looking back at your formative years, as a child and a young person, what were the three events in your family's life and generally, which shaped the most who you are and your values? Given that your children will not have had the same experiences, how might their values and priorities be different?*

Stepping Back To Go Forward

Family prosperity planning is about stepping back and taking a holistic and strategic approach to the family. Most families are so focused on making money and succeeding in business that they forget to take the time to create a shared vision for the future of all the wealth that they have created.

The most successful businesses in the world all have an inspiring purposeful vision that has the buy-in of all its stakeholders – the directors, the employees, and the shareholders. Yet families fall short of creating a similar vision for themselves.

How can you possibly create a legacy when the future is so unclear? Families that fail, do so because they do not understand the business of being a family. Once you have created a certain amount of wealth, you cannot rely on hope or luck to ensure that you keep it for multiple generations.

*'It requires a great deal of boldness and a great deal of caution
to make a great fortune, and when you have got it,
it requires ten times more wit to keep it.'*
Nathan Rothschild

If your intention is to achieve multi-generational financial success, then you need to apply the same principles for your family that you do in business. Therefore, question where you want to be in the future and what your intentions are for the family in twenty, fifty, and even one hundred years into the future. This should go beyond the financial goals that you set yourself as a family.

Creating a vision for the family is not something that you do once, and thereafter it is done. It needs to be shared, refreshed, and fine-tuned as the family and its circumstances evolve. That is why there is a need to have regular conversations amongst the family, whoever you consider it to be.

But also, life changes.

Births, marriages, divorces, and death all alter the composition of who the family is. Each generational transfer has the capacity to lead to a re-ordering of the family's priorities. The business environment in which families operate, communities in which they live, and societal norms similarly never stand still and invariably make their imprint on the family's values and vision for the future.

More immediately, just because a child has no interest today in running the family business does not mean that they should be counted out indefinitely. It may be that in three years' time, after they have gone out into the big wide world and worked for someone else, they may have secured the skillset, desire, and ambition to be part of and take over the running of the family business. The temporal aspect is very important because nothing is set in stone.

Senior generations should be astute enough not to close the door for their children to re-join the family business at a time when they are better equipped to make a valuable contribution and have the commitment to do so.

Family members who have worked externally and subsequently decide that they do want to be part of the family enterprise tend to come with a very new commitment, which is entirely different because it is their choice. It is also very likely that they will bring new ideas which can be greatly beneficial to the business and even vital for its success. In fact, we have seen that certain families insist that family members must prove themselves by working and succeeding in unrelated businesses before being invited to work for the family business, particularly where they are looking to join in a leadership capacity. This is called meritocracy and provides much-needed balance to the age-old family problem of nepotism.

Likewise, the next generation typically sees external experiences as adding credibility to what they can bring to the family. That gives them a voice, which they believe they would not have had, had they just grown incrementally within the business and with the business.

It should also be recognised that the next generation members can bring fresh ideas, examples of best practices from the industry, and an understanding of new technologies. They are also much more likely to be value-driven in their careers, investment choices, and approaches to business, which can help the family to incorporate Environmental, Social, and Governance (ESG) issues into its business and investment strategy. With consumers and regulatory focus on ESG increasing exponentially, and companies that demonstrate good corporate governance and social responsibility being more likely to command premium prices for their products, services and share prices, this can prove invaluable to the success of the family business in the long-term.

The role of next generation thinking in future-proofing the family business should not be underestimated.

But the key obstacle for many families will be the existence of family dynamics which expect the continued success of the family to come from those who have created its wealth in the first place. Also, how do you get over the fact that wealth creators struggle to let go of control?

Senior generations, therefore, need to be encouraged to see that businesses must combine both continuity and innovation to be able to adapt and succeed, whereas next generation leaders cannot develop the "entrepreneurial muscle" without being given the space and a canvass to leave their own mark on. ESG and digital technologies may be just that opportunity.

Your thoughts:

- *Are you encouraging your children to branch out and acquire qualifications, expertise, and skills externally, or are you worried about the possibility of them doing that and never returning to the family business?*

- *How would you like the next generation to engage with, and contribute to, the family business or family/investment office?*

- *Have you discussed with your children their thoughts and wishes regarding remaining involved with the family business or family office and potentially leading it, alone or with their siblings?*

- *What will it take for you to be persuaded that the next generation is leadership-ready?*

- *How are you preparing the next generation for responsibility within the family businesses and structures?*

Letting Go

This can be a really difficult issue to get over – especially for the first generation.

In this regard, it is important to appreciate the mindset of the first generation. They usually come from a modest background and have worked exceptionally hard to build a business from scratch and establish an element of success and wealth, making huge sacrifices in the process so that their children would experience a better life. Most of the time, their lives and sometimes identities are tied to the business they have founded.

This explains why it can be such an enormous hurdle for many of them to let go of control, even where there is an intellectual understanding that they need to. In practice, it does not happen so readily, or sometimes at all, during the lifetime of the founder.

We often have discussions with families regarding at what stage the next generation should be brought in on the conversation.

Case Study: The 300-Year Plan

A preeminent family governance expert once talked about how, as part of her role in a single-family office, her early conversations with the principal regarding governance went.

She kept repeatedly asking the principal, 'So when are you going to speak to the next generation?'

Each time the principal would say, 'Do I have to? Why do I have to?'

At that point, she would invariably bring the principal back to his stated objective: To keep the family together and the business prospering for the next three hundred years.

So, every time he would ask, 'Why do I have to?' she would answer, 'Remind me, what is your objective?'

'To keep the family together and keep the business prosperous for the next three hundred years.'

'That is why you must get the next generation involved and let go.'

And that same conversation – almost as a broken record – would happen every now and again until eventually, one day, that penny-dropping moment happened.

'Hmm, but of course, if I don't have that conversation, then how is that vision going to happen?'

Sometimes, all that it takes is to regularly remind the first generation about their vision and objectives for the penny to finally drop. It is a matter of time and patience.

The more often that conversation takes place, and the more advisors around the family who raise the same issue at different points in time, the more likely the senior generation can one day come to realise that, of course, unless I do that, I am not equipping the next generation to lead. So how can I expect them to suddenly rise to the challenge when I am not there or, worse still, if I am incapacitated.

Incapacitation is an issue that most families do not consider or talk about at all. They talk about it even less than death.

Statistically, there are so many families who will be touched by that issue at one point or another. And when the issue of incapacity concerns leaders within businesses, within business families, that can be both devastating and leave the next generation completely unprepared for that eventuality.

Their senior family member is still there; they have not departed, and the family must now tread around the issue extremely carefully, given the onset of incapacity is often not acknowledged and sometimes vehemently denied by the family member affected.

There are many risks that, if the senior generation talked about and considered realistically with their advisors, they would realise that it is essential for there to be some form of gradual transfer of governance, not just of wealth.

The emphasis must be on 'gradual.' Nobody expects the kind of giving up of control to happen overnight. In fact, that would not be wise either.

Ideally, families and their current leaders should engage in co-governance for a reasonable period, whereby the necessary transfer of human and intellectual capital to the next generation can take place. This process involves both current and future leaders being concurrently involved in the family businesses, working together on projects in practice, not just theory, and ensuring that the ship is steady when the time comes for the guard to change.

Your thoughts:

- *Is there a contingency plan in place for the succession to key roles within the family business, family office, Private Trust Companies, and investment or protector committees?*

- *If so, do these extend to the situation of permanent or temporary incapacity of key individuals? How is that defined?*

- *Who is the arbiter of whether a relevant contingency has been triggered?*

- *Have those earmarked to assume specified roles as part of any contingency planning been inducted to allow them to be effective in the role immediately if required? Do they have the necessary information? Do they know who to contact in terms of external advisers?*

The Heir Apparent

It is exceptionally valuable to be able to train, support, and mentor your child - whether it is your son or daughter, or another relative - to become the next CEO of the business, lead the family office or assume other positions of responsibility within the family structures. That process takes, on average, at least five to ten years.

Transitioning is a long process.

It is not just about them taking on the roles and responsibilities of the office; it is also about ensuring that all the stakeholders - shareholders, directors, employees and other family members - are involved in facilitating that transition.

To avoid accusations of nepotism, it is essential that the family's chosen next business leader, being a family member, wins over the stakeholders in the business. Whilst the practice of allocating leadership roles to family members should not always be seen as having a negative connotation - after all, which family does not want to see the next generation takeover the family business - it is essential that the family members' eligibility for leadership is balanced by a system of meritocracy in terms of their selection for such roles.

Effectively, the next generation must earn the right to take over the business leadership.

Case Study: C. Hoare & Co Private Bank's Approach To Family Leaders

This is currently the oldest family-run bank in the world. It was founded in 1672 and is approximately one hundred years older than the Rothschilds dynasty.

The current Board of Directors and its shareholders are still family members, an amazing three hundred years after the bank was founded. One of the reasons for their success is that they use meritocracy when choosing family Board members. Every director on their current Board had to have a background working for another private bank for several years before becoming eligible to become a director of C. Hoare & Co.

Choosing successors can be easy when you have a pool of over one thousand family members! However, what happens if you are first-generation, and you only have two children to choose from or as your successor?

Credibility is key when choosing, supporting and training the next business leader. The successor wants to be respected as a capable leader of the business and not be seen as simply having the right bloodline. It is essential that the handover process is done during the incumbent's lifetime and not forced upon their successor because of sudden, unexpected death.

The successor will have to demonstrate their capacity and ability to lead, including the desire to learn from those already involved in the business. They will have to earn the respect of both family members and other stakeholders. They must also be allowed to make their own mistakes and implement their own ideas, as this is part of the learning process. Whilst the success of any business is not guaranteed, implementing a well thought-out and structured succession plan is key to ensuring that the business does not fail!

While there is usually a mechanism for including the next generation in the family business, what if they are not the most capable or appropriate persons for the role? What if they have no desire to take over the family business?

Every child has the right to follow their own path towards happiness. It is essential that the needs of every family member are discussed regularly in a forum that is safe and encourages effective communication.

Your thoughts:

- *Does your family have a forum where you meet up regularly to discuss the needs of each individual and that of the family as a collective?*

- *Has your family ever discussed business leadership succession in terms of planning for the boards of family businesses, the family office, Private Trust Companies and other key roles within family structures (such as protectors and membership of investment committees)?*

- *Is there a formal qualification criterion and process for consulting on and selecting family member leaders?*

- *How do these processes ensure that no branch of the family gets disenfranchised?*

- *What processes are there for board refreshment?*

- *What checks and balances are there to ensure a fair distribution of decision-making power and influence and accountability within the family and its structures?*

Automatic Privileges?

While succession to businesses that lie at the heart of the family's wealth is clearly fundamental to the future success and prosperity of the family, there are many more questions that business families need to have a position on. For example:

- Will family members have preferential treatment within the organisation? Or will they be treated just like any other employee?

- Will they be required to 'start at the bottom' and work their way up the corporate ladder, or will they be made a director from day one?

- What qualifications and continuing development require-ments will apply with respect to board roles to be assumed by family members?

- Will, to the extent possible, siblings be allocated comparable roles in terms of status, remuneration and benefits?

- How does the family balance the desire to ensure that no family branch becomes disenfranchised with the reality that leadership capacity is unevenly distributed?

The answer to these questions can vary depending on which region or culture your family comes from or lives in.

If you take the Middle East, for example, there is the desire for family members to be remunerated, at a minimum, on a market rate basis but more preferably, more generously, purely because they are family members.

This is as valid an approach as any other, but it is important for it to be discussed. It needs to be something that the family consciously chooses to do. A family should not sleepwalk into an organisational or operational setup whereby nobody has consciously decided that a particular approach is agreed upon, acceptable, or appropriate.

That reinforces the benefit, again, of having regular, candid, and open communications and a forum in which they can take place.

The same applies to any other aspect of family governance.

Part 3

Planning For The What If's

Expect Trouble If ...

Regular communication within the family and with other stakeholders in the business. How valuable is it? Invaluable.

Engaging in meaningful discussions about contingency and continuity planning should happen sooner rather than later. The importance of this is nowhere more evident than in families where the incumbent leader is forced to relinquish control of the family business through incapacitation or due to their premature demise.

Families are typically advised to expect the best but prepare for the worst. They should never wait for disaster to strike before taking action. Prevention is always better than finding a cure.

Take the mining industry as an example.

The equipment used on most mining sites can run into the tens and hundreds of millions of dollars. It is an industry-standard to have planned and scheduled maintenance shutdowns to perform preventative maintenance. The worst-case scenario is an unplanned, unscheduled shutdown. On some sites, the cost of dealing with such an eventuality starts from a million dollars a day for the duration of any downtime.

A site without preventative maintenance or a crisis management plan is a very costly malfunction waiting to happen.

Family wealth is the same. You need to proactively plan. Families do not plan to fail; they simply fail to plan.

One or more of retirement, ill health, diminished capacity or incapacity and ultimately death is statistically inevitable. We may not like this inevitability but given the scale of wealth and the high cost of getting it wrong, it is prudent and beneficial long term for families to have difficult conversations about the what if's early and put contingency planning in place. Like preventative maintenance, it just makes good sense. It starts with regular conversations and will ultimately build towards great family governance.

This type of conversation is even more important when there are family businesses at the heart of the family's wealth.

How valuable would it be to you, as the next generation in line to take over the family business, to have your father or your mother or other senior family members holding your hand, advising and mentoring you for the next five to ten years or however long it takes, while you learn about the family business and develop your leadership potential?

Rather than, *I am sorry, mother or father passed away. Off you go! You are now the CEO of this business. You have no experience or expertise, but good luck, because your parents made you the next in line.*

The issue of unplanned succession can be exacerbated when two or more siblings are involved in the family business, but the parents have not undertaken the process of identifying, let alone preparing for the role of the next business leader. After all, you cannot have two CEOs in the same company! Just remember the story of the Ambani brothers. Their rivalry destroyed their family relationship, broke up the family business, and caused the bankruptcy of one of the brothers. Was this the family legacy their father envisaged?

Getting the process right of choosing the next business leader from within the family, who has the personal qualities and has built up the necessary experience and knowledge to both successfully run the business and maintain the unity of the family, can and will be hugely beneficial to both the family business and well-being of the family as a whole.

When the strategy of choosing a successor for the family business is formulated and executed correctly, the business will continue to grow and be successful for multiple generations. There are countless examples, such as C. Hoare & Co Private Bank, that prove how invaluable it is to future plan, have great governance structures and maintain excellent lines of communication amongst the family members.

So, whilst the theory and the idealistic vision is that every family will work together and learn from the senior generations and bring in a bit of their own skills, insights, and vision for the future, too many families are still struggling with the basic communication process to allow this to happen.

What families should work toward is having regular, structured communications. Family members should be encouraged to bring out their concerns and discuss them openly with the rest of the family. Even if you do not reach an agreement on every issue but occasionally agree to disagree, that ability to have a frank discussion is incredibly valuable and, in terms of family members, helps to build the confidence to initiate or engage in such communications.

But not every family is able to achieve this on its own, and so it is the trusted advisers around them whose skill and commitment are needed to encourage and facilitate the family's development of improved communication habits.

Sadly, most families do not appreciate the problem that they face and, even worse, do not have a clear vision for the family's future, which means that having focused, constructive discussions becomes even more challenging for them.

As previously mentioned, the sad statistic is that *70% of all wealthy families will fail financially over just two generations, and this increases to more than 90% over three generations.* Lack of communication is a major contributing cause.

Many families find it difficult to have these types of conversations without allowing their emotions to take control.

> *'If you cannot control your emotions, don't ever expect to control money.'*
>
> Warren Buffet

If your family struggles to manage the emotional charge that comes with family discussions within the existing family dynamic, then having a third-party mediator facilitate these conversations is vital for the success and unity of the family. You cannot build without having strong foundations and most strong foundations are based on effective, regular communication amongst the family members. It is always easier to have these conversations when the trust still exists amongst the family.

Equally, where disagreement has dented the family's ability to trust and be open with each other, waiting for the family relationship to implode or simply relying on luck or the passage of time to resolve these challenges is not a strategy that we would ever recommend.

Family Retreats Or Families Retreat

If it is so important to mediate emotional interactions, how do families balance themselves given the multiple roles they have as business owners, directors/managers and family members, all in one go?

How do they balance their various roles and responsibilities, and how should they?

It is important for families to be able to step outside of their immediate, day-to-day roles.

Sometimes they do that in a deliberately created forum, such as a family retreat. This typically involves the family meeting in a neutral location. They would usually start with a form of family-building experience before moving on to serious discussions. That may be the opportunity they need to rebalance.

Other families may be more used to organically managing those different hats that they wear and roles that they perform; for example, they may be discussing issues that their business faces at the dinner table, with children soaking in those conversations without ever realising that these are business decisions, given the overlap between family and business.

Whatever the family's approach, essentially, it is all about identifying potential issues pertaining to any of the family members' roles and nipping them in the bud. Unless this is done and early enough, you are likely to see family conflicts play out in the boardroom.

If there is a little niggle here and there, so long as that can be expressed and given an outlet, the family can work with it.

Indeed, it does not matter whether one is faced with is a minor niggle between family members, or a more significant issue, affecting the family members as business owners, such as a strategy for the extraction of value or the re-investment of profits – in either case, it is essential to deal with such matters as soon as the issue manifests itself, to ensure it is resolved early on. Disregarding issues as unimportant allows the problem to grow unchecked and fester. This can be as destructive as ignoring a cancer tumour within your body. When it is small, it can be easily removed, but allowing it to grow will kill your family!

Unfortunately, a lot of families have got blind spots for those issues or are simply too scared of the consequences to deal with them as soon as they appear on the radar.

Typically, when you talk to a family about family governance for the first time, they will tell you what a happy family they are – and they probably are, on many levels. But if you talk to each of the family members individually, you will soon realise that there are underlying issues waiting to turn into problems if they are not addressed.

Sometimes they can be quite small things and easy to resolve at that point. It could be about the holiday home and whether all children have got equal access to it during the summer months when everybody wants to be there! These small issues, unless discussed, can and will eventually be misinterpreted and turned into something bigger, such as, 'mother and father favour my sibling.'

The issue and how parents deal with it could be and often is, made to be about love. It could be made to mean something completely different from what the parent is thinking, but because there is no communication, everyone interprets it - or more often misinterprets it - into something that can easily escalate into a full-blown conflict, especially after a parent's death.

Communication - we keep coming back to that one word!

The goal is to consider the family members' different roles, to identify issues that are present today and have the capacity to grow into a dispute if left unaddressed, and resolve them before they do. The challenge is to recognize their destructive potential and accord them the importance they deserve despite the numerous other issues which the family will be facing at the same time, which may seem more important or urgent.

Family disputes are rarely born overnight, with no prior indication. Dark clouds gather first before a torrential downpour. Not noticing that a storm is building could mean that the family vessel is put at risk when it could have been safely pulled to shore, had the crew been paying attention.

This is not a new dynamic! Family wealth creation - and conflicts over family wealth - have been around for centuries. We know that both ancient Babylonian and Egyptian families were arguing over inter-generational family wealth issues!

Your thoughts:

- *Has your family experienced conflict?*

- *If so, do you think, with the benefit of hindsight, that the tell-tale signs of dissatisfaction had been apparent earlier?*

- *What action could the family have taken to prevent the issue from escalating into a dispute?*

- *If your family is fortunate enough not to have experienced serious discord, do you have any concerns as to what life, the family office, the family business, and family relations might look like when your parents are no longer there to hold the family together? Have you discussed these with your parents, siblings, and trusted advisers?*

- *What might be the pressure lines that the family faces in the future, given the family members' different personalities, aspirations and involvement in the decision-making for the family business, office, and/or structures?*

Strike Three

Forbes magazine, Merrill Lynch, and the Money magazine each cite research that looks at the fate of substantial family fortunes over the last three centuries and highlights the following damning statistics:

- … 75% of a family's wealth is still created and owned by the first generation.
- 70% of a family's wealth will fall over within two generations.
- That statistic climbs sharply beyond 90% when the wealth reaches three generations.

This clearly demonstrates the challenge of retaining wealth for multiple generations. So, what can families do about it?

It is true that many second and third generations end up ultimately spending and dissipating the family's wealth unless something is put in place to address that likelihood.

We know that the first generation is the people with the entrepreneurial genius, the incidence of which (even within the same family) is rarer than one might think. So, the probability of the next generation comprising even one more such business genius is actually not that high.

We also know that choosing a successor is not an easy task – it is often coloured by cultural and family traditions and not always, or necessarily, aptitude. There are often unspoken and sometimes disappointed expectations that lead senior generations to opt for an alternative business leader to what might have been their choice. With senior generations remaining productive and in leadership roles or control of assets longer, the next generations will often be old before there are wealthy. This could mean that a successor designate predeceases their parent, leaving an unexpected void. And there are, of course, those families in which choosing a successor is simply a taboo topic. None of these situations assist the next generation in retaining and growing the family's wealth for future generations.

How the next generation behaves around money often depends on whether they arrived at a time when the first generation was still building, or maybe they came at a time when wealth had been achieved and was just normal – what children have always known, and so they do not have the same kind of hunger and ambition as their parents.

It is important to recognize that each generation will be shaped by their own unique experiences and what knowledge, expertise and stories have been passed down to them.

You cannot expect a second or third generation family member to necessarily understand the perspective of the first generation unless that has been discussed. Even then, it is impossible for them to fully appreciate the sacrifices that the first generation had to make to become successful.

'These are all the difficulties that we faced when we were building the business. This is what spurred us on and what motivated us to keep on going. Mistakes were made, and lessons were learned, and, in the end, sheer determination resulted in abundance.'

So, passing on the family story can be very inspiring and invaluable for the next generation.

Case Study: The Importance of Passing Down the Family Story

One of the families that Antoaneta worked with was asked to put together a draft of the family story for discussion and to ultimately include it in the family constitution. The father went away and wrote a few sentences.

What came back was dry, brief, and strictly factual. It did not give anyone much to go on. So, she asked the father to reflect on what were some of the defining moments for the family and in establishing the family business. He came back with a few paragraphs.

This was an improvement, but again, it failed to convey much that was personal or give any insight into what it was that had made the family who they are today. So, Antoaneta sent the father away one last time, asking him to dig deeper for what it is that he would like to pass to his heirs. He eventually came back with three pages on the family's story.

Having read that – much more self-reflective and emotionally evocative – story, she looked at her client in the eyes and said, 'You know what? I'm not your daughter, but even I am inspired.'

He then admitted that the more he kept writing, the more he realised that he had not passed the family story to his children, let alone to his grandchildren.

This is what we mean by passing down the family's intellectual capital to the next generation!

Helping families realise the value of capturing the family's wealth creation stories – stories that are engrained in the senior generation's approach to life, business and wealth and which they assume children will somehow absorb by osmosis – can trigger those penny-dropping moments that are essential if the family is to retain its unity and entrepreneurial zest over the generations.

Once a family reaches the conclusion that this exercise has value, that they need to do something, then they are very capable of doing it, they know how to go about telling the family's story in a way that touches and inspires, and the results are invaluable.

The challenge is getting families to appreciate the value of what might seem like an odd exercise that the adviser has asked them to do, which, being diligent people, they are willing to oblige.

The question that families do not necessarily express but ask themselves initially is, 'Why am I doing this?'

But once they understand the value, invariably, they really pour their energy, enthusiasm and skill into stories that help their vision for the family to come through.

It is wonderful when the whole family is involved in this process and participates in building the family wealth narrative together.

When a young person is inspired, they will come and pester their parents for the answers. 'And what happened then, mum? What did you and dad do then?' How often is it that parents struggle to get their children to listen? Might this be because what parents are sharing are the dry, uninspiring canons for a successful life, devoid of the emotional connection that is needed for children to choose to follow them?

The most successful families that have survived and thrived for multiple generations are those that plan for and manage to pass all their wealth to their next generation, including their family story – the human, intellectual, social, and family capital and certainly not just the financial capital.

Stories that inspire enable family members to appreciate the wealth and where it came from.

Once you know where it came from and how hard your predecessors had worked to create that wealth, children become inspired to ensure that the wealth lasts for multiple generations.

Your thoughts:

- *Have you been told your family's story?*
- *How does it feed into the family's personal and business values?*
- *What qualities inspire you in the senior generation and your predecessors?*
- *How would you like to contribute to the family's story and legacy?*
- *Have you conveyed the family's story to your children and grandchildren?*

NICHOLAS CHARLES & ANTOANETA PROCTOR

PART 4

Sustainable Philanthropy And Relationships

Why Giving Back Works
For Wealthy Families

We have discovered that based on their appreciation of the value of wealth, families naturally start to consider giving back. They ask, 'How important is it, therefore, for us, as a wealthy family, to have a sustainable philanthropic arm?'

Philanthropy is a valuable and key aspect of family governance because that is where you can really see the family's values translated into practical projects and solutions.

As a starting point, it is essential for families to consider and elicit their core values. Both their values as individuals and their collective values as a family. You can list them on a piece of paper.

As part of promoting effective communication within a family, we always undertake a values elicitation exercise amongst all the family members. We have discovered that all human beings will listen if they are spoken to in their own values, and if you wish to communicate effectively with the rest of your family, then you must link your values to those of the person or persons you are communicating with.

Understanding each family member's individual values is vital and will help to build family values that are authentic and not a collection of fancy words that nobody truly believes in.

The value of purpose-driven philanthropy for families is manyfold.

It creates a space for a purpose greater than the individual needs of each family member to emerge. It also creates a collective responsibility around the family's wealth because there is a binding purpose, the fulfilment of which relies on the family's continuing commitment to gift, fund raise, and contribute its enthusiasm, skills and social capital.

It unites families by rallying the members of different generations and within the same generation around an inspiring project or a collection of projects; it gives them the opportunity to work together as a family and, through that, to experience communication as equals, outside the hierarchy of existing family structures.

Philanthropy provides a valuable learning experience, which everyone can then take and transpose onto any other area of their family life. In particular, the sustainability of a charitable cause provides experience to family members of disciplined financial management, which should help ensure that their personal projects and entrepreneurial endeavours do not end up as bottomless pits that engulf all their wealth or a substantial proportion of it. These are lessons that can be transferred to the family members' business and investment decision-making.

Purposeful philanthropy facilitates conversations and communication amongst the family members, which are vital to the long-term success of the family. It also brings in those members of the family who are not interested in investments, tax planning and maybe even the family business. It creates interest in stewarding the family's wealth to enable it to be deployed with impact and instils a greater sense of responsibility and prudence.

It is an incredibly powerful tool.

Families with a sustainable philanthropic arm are inspired to ensure that it is as successful as possible because now the wealth is no longer about the individuals. It is about something bigger, something more important than individual needs, which is why it is so important to have one. It is not a coincidence that families who have achieved multi-generational financial success all have a sustainable philanthropic arm to the family's wealth.

Your thoughts:

- *Do you and your family appreciate the important role philanthropy has when it comes to retaining the family wealth for multiple generations?*

- *Have you sat with your family and discussed setting up a philanthropic arm?*

- *What and where are you inspired as a family to make a difference on this planet?*

- *Who within your family would enjoy having the responsibility of running the family's philanthropic affairs?*

What Makes A Good Beneficiary?

There are a few components to that.

The first and most important is understanding the purpose of the family's wealth or a particular structure through which it is held, depending on whether you are looking at family members as beneficiaries of structures established for their benefit (a trust child) or as the beneficiaries of the family's wealth in the wider sense.

The second aspect is the willingness to engage with the wider stakeholders. In the context of a trust structure, this means the willingness to engage with the trustees and not to look upon them as them and us. Trustees are often seen by children as an unnecessary hurdle to their getting their inheritance – 'Why did mum simply not give me my share?'; as someone who is there to restrict what they, as beneficiaries, want to do. This can create an unhelpful dynamic, whereby trustees who are seeking to protect beneficiaries from themselves and other risks while fulfilling the requirements of the trust deed and having regard for the settlor's wishes are being seen by beneficiaries as an adversary.

A good beneficiary is someone who has the curiosity to ask questions of their trustees and professional advisers, who seeks to understand the settlor's perspective (why they felt it important to create a structure instead of making absolute gifts), and who is open to engaging in frank discussions, transparently. It is important that beneficiaries take an interest in the structures - how the trust assets are invested, if income is being generated, how the administration costs associated with the structure are being met, whether trust assets have appreciated in value, etc. These are all aspects that impact how the trust fund can be deployed to benefit its beneficiaries and accommodate their varying needs. Unless a beneficiary has an appreciation of these factors, unrealistic expectations can arise, which have the potential to deplete the trust fund if left unchecked or pit them against the trustees, whose role is to preserve the trust fund for future generations.

Keeping oneself informed and taking responsibility by talking to all those relevant people - be that advisors, trustees, or family members – should enable requests that you make to be seen as reasonable and capable of being accommodated.

It is also important to frame your communications as requests rather than demands, whether you are addressing the trustees of a family structure or the family. Getting their support for what you wish to do will typically involve a discussion, maybe a business plan, and certainly convincing them that what you are asking for is in your best interests. In the process of discussing and communicating with the relevant stakeholders, one may get what one asked for, or something different may emerge from that discussion. But one should not assume their entitlement. Approaching such conversations with an open mind is another important component of being a good beneficiary.

Being imbued from a young age with the family's story about where the wealth came from and the sacrifices that senior generations went through should also assist in family members appreciating the benefits of a family structure which helps them preserve that wealth.

We should also add the need for families to focus on bringing up children who share a mindset.

Next generation family members are not just beneficiaries; they are stewards of the family's wealth and legacy, and this is an important responsibility.

Each beneficiary will be a part of building the family's legacy and ensuring that it endures for multiple generations. The more involved the rising generations are, the more they can feel that they are shaping that legacy and that they are there to contribute and give something back.

Your thoughts:

- *Does your family have an education process in place to ensure that the next generation appreciates the family wealth and the responsibility that comes with it?*

- *Have you discussed with your children the reason for, and the importance of, setting up trusts or other wealth holding structures to protect and manage the family's assets?*

- *Have you introduced the trustees and wider professional advisory team to the next generation? If so, how often do the next generation accompany you when you meet up with them?*

- *How often do you and your trustees discuss the family investments and structures with the next generation – quarterly, annually, or never?*

Family Banks

Drawing on the insights of:

James E. Hughes, Jr. Esq. author of Family Wealth: Keeping It in the Family, and

Family: The Compact Among Generations and

Linda Davis Taylor in The Family Bank: A Strategy for Preserving Wealth

http://www.cliffordswan.com/blog/the-family-bank-a-strategy-for-preserving-wealth

'Be careful to leave your sons well instructed rather than rich, for the hopes of the instructed are better than the wealth of the ignorant.'

Epictetus, Greek philosopher

A 'family bank' is a concept that is aimed at fairly supporting the growth and development of family members and their aspirations without creating a sense of entitlement.

The purpose of the family bank is to encourage entrepreneurialism, help develop the human and intellectual capital of family members, as well as their independence, and cultivate responsible behaviours around money.

Other benefits of a family bank are that a lending (rather than gifting) strategy can help protect assets that the family members may lose otherwise - because of inexperience and over-optimism, insufficient due diligence and vetting of potential new investments, poor management, changes within the household such as divorce, or indecision and/or disagreement about asset allocation or how assets are managed.

Whilst, not a formal bank, it is usually a separate entity or trust that is set up by senior generations to provide constructive financial assistance to the next and future generations in the form of loans. Instead of simply giving money to family members and risking a dependency culture developing, the family bank loans funds to them, having utilised a formal process to assess the viability of projects they are intended to pay for.

Under a family bank arrangement, funding is mainly provided to support investments that are likely to increase the family's financial wealth (such as the setting up of a new business) or help preserve wealth for future generations through investment in them.

According to James E. Hughes, Jr. Esq, there are essentially two types of loans that a family bank would (or indeed should) provide – investment loans and enhancement loans.

The Investment Loan

The purpose of this type of loan is to ultimately increase the family's wealth by supporting financially remunerative endeavours by the next generation members, such as the starting of a new business. In this way, the budding entrepreneur can overcome the lack of early-stage external funding and establish their own business, oftentimes under the family's mentorship, which the family member can then grow, while repaying the family with interest in return for their help. The family bank may also choose to take a minority equity stake in the new business, which may increase the family's risk if the business fails but will also increase its returns if the business is a success.

Investment loans can also be made to support educational purposes that provide or enhance the professional skills and managerial capabilities of family members, on the basis that such loans are likely to increase the individual's earning power.

An investment loan is a key component in fostering an entrepreneurial spirit - that same spirit that created the wealth in the first place and is required to ensure its continued growth but which many families struggle to maintain the further removed their members become from the original wealth creator.

To create a supportive environment for the next generations to grow their entrepreneurial muscle, they need to be allowed to make their own mistakes. Being encouraged to experiment and develop their own innovative ideas is hugely important - even if those ideas occasionally fail, provided family members learn from those mistakes.

Being supported in the pursuit of their own ideas also gives the rising generation the feeling that they have the freedom to fly out and "do their own thing." This breeds independence, greater financial awareness, and appreciation for the family and its structures, which are seen as championing the individual family members.

Case Study: Sir Stelios Haji-Ioannou

When Stelios left the family business, Troodos Shipping, to set up his own business, he managed to 'negotiate' a payment of $30 million from his father, Loucas. The only condition that his father placed on him was that he wanted his two siblings to benefit from any financial success because the money represented 'family wealth and not your own.'

The business created was called Stelmar Shipping, and Stelios managed to successfully grow the business until it eventually went public on the New York Stock Exchange in 2001.

In 1995, two years after founding Stelmar, Stelios utilised another $7.5 million of family funds to start a low-cost airline called EasyJet. Despite starting with only two leased aircraft, he successfully grew the business until it was floated on the London Stock Exchange in November 2000. Currently, he and his two siblings are the largest shareholders of the company, which in 2021 was valued at £4.64 billion.

Stelios continues to run multiple businesses using the Easy brand.

Although this is not a classic case of utilising a family bank, this story does provide a backdrop of what can be achieved when the family supports and embraces the entrepreneurial visions of the next generation.

Family members should not be tied down to doing something they cannot feel passionate about and so do not wish to spend a lifetime doing. Equally, the pursuit of personal happiness requires the next generation to have the courage of their convictions and follow their dreams.

Knowing that their elders have their backs can be really empowering, though.

There is nothing wrong with failing as part of growing. Once you do, you realize... *'It wasn't that bad. I'm still alive, and I now know what I need to do to prevail. I'm going to take those learnings and transform them into a blueprint for success.'*

Make mistakes, provided you fail forward, because this can be an exceptionally beneficial learning curve and a springboard to your next successful venture; because we are yet to meet a successful entrepreneur who has never once failed.

Failure is almost a necessary part of achieving success, and the truth is, most wealth is almost always built on a lot of failures.

Thomas Edison is the most famous example of this. As an inventor, he is said to have 'failed' a thousand times before he eventually discovered the lightbulb.

If we do not allow the next generation to fail, how on earth will they learn? It is an invaluable experience that builds character, commercial realism, and the capacity to lead.

The Enhancement Loan

This type of loan can support the family's long-term wealth preservation objectives if it increases the human or intellectual capital of its members and contributes to their well-being and a sense of purpose. Although they do not add directly to the financial capital of the family, such loans can be invaluable if they empower the next generation to utilise their own talents in a productive and meaningful way. Examples can include educational and self-improvement programmes being paid for through such loans.

As is the case in relation to gifts, fairness of process and outcome is essential in the disbursement of funds by the family bank to avoid the wealth being destructive to relationships. The family bank must be very clear about what element of the support provided is a loan to the family member with an expectation of repayment, what is an investment, and what is, in effect, a conditional gift where the loan will be forgiven in specified circumstances.

Any investment into the child's business is a risk for the family - if the business does well, the family benefits, but if the business fails, the family suffers the loss. Unless there is a strong business case for making such investments and robust processes for financial management are put in place, a perception of unequal treatment can arise.

It is therefore essential that formal rules and protocols are established, which bind all family members who wish to avail themselves of and secure the backing of the family bank. Examples of such rules could include the following:

- the family member who is the potential borrower must provide a business plan and loan application in the same way as a third-party commercial lender would expect to receive.

- the potential borrower is required to pitch their business idea to the bank's trustees.

- the loan, if granted, will stipulate the terms on which it is given, including its term, events of default, rate of interest and security (if any).

- the borrowing family member would be expected to provide periodic reports to the bank's trustees on progress and agreed Key Performance Indicators for the investment, and

- the family member will be expected to repay the loan. Express rules should be adopted regarding how the bank would deal with default on the loan, as well as whether and, if so, in what circumstances loans can be forgiven.

The good news is that, very often, there will be senior family members, acting as mentors or trusted advisors, who will work with the applicant family member in developing their business plan before it is agreed upon as ready for submission – *That looks like a great idea!*; who will help stress test the assumptions that underpin the business case, work out the numbers, and finetune the financial forecasts.

In that sense, there is learning before the family member has even started - before they even make the request for funding for the investment.

Equally, the application process gives another opportunity for the family to work together in a more 'open architecture' way, in the sense that family members are not tied to the existing family businesses and structures but are free to explore their own ideas whilst having the family on their side, facilitating something new to emerge.

You never know what such collaboration may eventually lead to.

A family bank encourages individual family members, next and future generations, to have the independence of thought and means to pursue their own creative ideas. This should assist in making the next generation feel part of the family, rather than needing to be the rebel who breaks away with tradition to follow their dreams and entrepreneurial vision.

But they must earn the right to be supported with funding from the family bank. They must come prepared and back their ideas with forecasted figures, a solid business case, and a business plan document. They must articulate those ideas as commercial propositions and expect to be 'grilled' about them for their viability. Just like they would be with any commercial bank.

As the applicant, the family member should expect to be held accountable throughout.

Family banks are usually created (in consultation with the family's tax and legal advisors) as trusts. As such, they will require the appointment of suitable trustees to administer loans and make decisions about loan applications.

The trustees will typically include a collection of family members and outside advisors who are financially savvy, knowledgeable, experienced in start-up investing, and capable of operating the family bank as a trust.

Linda Davis Taylor summarises some of the practices that families have adopted when setting up family banks as follows:

- Purpose – this should be clearly explained to all family members, both borrowers, and the family bank trustees. The family bank is essentially there to support productive activities via loans to family members.

- Privacy and confidentiality – all dealings with the family bank must remain private within the family and its trusted advisor group.

- Governance – each family is unique and therefore must decide how it wishes to manage its bank. The purpose and philosophy must be clearly communicated to family members in a written mission statement.

- Formal processes – what are the procedures for receiving and processing loan applications?

- Transparency – subject to privacy and confidentiality for certain financial information disclosed in the loan application, the purpose and amount of loans should generally be communicated to the family. This provides accountability for the borrower and communicates fairness to all family members as to how family resources will be made available.

A well-conceived family bank provides hands-on financial education for next generation family members, which is challenging yet supportive, especially in conjunction with the mentoring process that precedes the submission of loan applications. Individual members have the opportunity to learn from each other as different projects are proposed, reported on periodically, and ultimately completed. Witnessing the creative process unfold can also encourage other family members to start their own businesses and take the risk.

Family wealth and family bonds grow together with a well-run family bank, which can act as an incubator for the family's new ventures and is conducive to maintaining sustainable family relationships over the long run.

Your thoughts:

- *Does your family currently operate a family bank, or does it simply provide funds whenever requested by its members? If so, how does it operate and how often are the governance structures of the family bank reviewed and improved upon?*

- *Who currently sits on the banking panel? How often are their roles reviewed? What is the process of election and re-election? Do any family members sit on the panel, or are these positions reserved strictly for independent third-party advisors or trustees?*

- *How strict are your processes when deciding which family business or project the family bank should invest in? How often do you review these processes?*

- *What procedures do you have in place when loans given to family members cannot be paid back?*

- *What communication is there within the family regarding funding provided through the family bank and reporting back to the family by the relevant family member who has benefited from such funding so that their learning becomes the family's learning?*

PART 5

The Role Of Advisors

Professional Advisors And Loops

The biggest problem faced by professional advisors is, in our view, being limited to whatever information is provided to them by their family members, which rarely gives them the full picture. It is frustrating because we have never met a professional advisor who can read people's minds. If you can, then please pass on this skill!

Although we joke about reading the client's mind, all great advisors must continually ask their clients the right questions on a consistent basis to ensure that all the relevant information has been supplied. The advice that professional advisers can give to a family will only ever be as good as the information they are provided with.

Sometimes it is about the adviser asking the right questions to elicit the relevant information from the client. After all, a client may not fully appreciate what information has a bearing on the answer to a question they have posed.

The more skilful the adviser is at asking the right questions, the more likely they will be able to provide advice that best meets their client's needs, including those that even the client does not yet know they have.

Referring to the earlier example where the clients came for inheritance tax advice, you will recall there was that one sentence which said: '...consider putting in place a family constitution.'

Although the family thought they needed inheritance tax advice, they wanted something that went significantly deeper, but they did not recognise this until they were told about it. It is the bigger picture thinking that broadens the value of the advice to that family and takes the relationship to the next level.

Both parties' benefit.

An advisor who thinks in a holistic way should also be enabling the family to see that there is a range of additional considerations that they may wish to concentrate on. The family might not necessarily take up the offer at first - because all you are doing is making an offer to them to engage with the issues - but the more their advisors raise that one topic, the more likely the family is to turn their attention to it at some point.

As advisors, we need to anticipate and be able to guide our clients to engage with specific and broader issues, including those they did not realise they had.

A lot of families do not appreciate that a problem exists... until the adviser explains what it is and why it is important to address it. They are looking for a solution to one problem, but they might have problems significantly bigger than they are aware of.

For example, poor communication underpins most of the governance challenges that wealthy families experience; but rarely will a client come seeking advice on communication. That is why it is so important that, as advisors, we ask our clients the right questions to attain that relevant information. Unfortunately, a lot of advisors are quite reactive and do not 'chase' the information proactively.

Usually, a client comes with a query. Often it is just a transactional query, and questions are asked to enable that transaction to take place. However, the more the advisor understands the wider context within which that query is being raised, the more they can tailor their advice, which then is more likely to be of value to that family.

Therefore, something as fundamental as the family's vision ought to be communicated to the advisory team, even where their current involvement is limited to a discrete transaction. After all, how can any advisor help you reach a destination that they do not know you are trying to reach, or assess whether a particular investment you are considering furthers the family's vision?

With any new client, there is a learning curve, whereby the advisor learns about the family... and the family learns how to be a good client by being open with their advisor, including respect for the contextual information and not just the details that the client thinks need to go into the transaction documents.

A key precondition to families being willing to share more with their advisers is that the adviser builds trust with the family. It is the advisor's responsibility to earn their clients' trust. However, trust takes years to earn and moments to lose.

Family prosperity is a long game and any advisor who wishes to make fast gains from the client relationship must be replaced. This may seem harsh, but when dealing with multi-generational prosperity planning, it is not uncommon for the work required to span upwards of twenty years and encompass the transition between two or more successive generations. How much information do you think your adviser needs to be able to fulfil such a mandate?

Your thoughts:

- *Do your current professional advisors share your focus on the long term when it comes to establishing your family's legacy?*

- *Do your advisers demonstrate curiosity and willingness to invest in getting to know the family inside out?*

- *Have you equipped your advisers with a solid understanding of your family's vision in order that they can advise you holistically and not merely on an ad hoc, transactional basis?*

Withholding Information – Deliberate Or Misconceived?

Drawing on the insights of Ray Lancaster in his post on Quora, *What does it mean to withhold information.*

Withholding information means that you deliberately hold back information from others to have more power than them. It takes several forms:

- holding back all the information.
- holding back part of the information; or
- sharing the information, but too late for it to be useful.

For example, if you discover a faster and cheaper way to solve a problem than your customers, you might:

- share that information with your colleagues for everyone, including all your customers, to profit from it; or
- withhold that information from colleagues to make your performance seem better than theirs.

In our experience, people who withhold information on a regular basis get found out. It might give them a temporary advantage in the short run, but even that temporary advantage will be discovered sooner or later.

When discovered, withholders typically claim that they:

- 'forgot' to share. One can give the benefit of the doubt once but never twice.

- did not know the information was that valuable. This can be seen as an admission of negligence in some circumstances, or

- were about to share but had not got around to it.

People with a reputation for withholding information do not survive long professionally. Their colleagues end up withholding information in return. The ensuing escalation is highly destructive.

The question then becomes, why do families withhold information from their advisors?

The answers are never as straightforward as one might expect, and often the client would not have even rationalised their decision to do so, but the reasons usually include one or more of the following:

- the client assumes that the information is not valuable or required – i.e., withholding information about foreign assets from their UK advisors;

- they do not trust their advisor with what they feel is sensitive information; or

- it is an honest mistake – for example, the client forgot about shares they owned in an overseas company.

Whatever the reason may be, it is always up to the advisor to consistently and regularly ask their client the relevant questions to ensure that they understand the full picture regarding the client's family, estate and requirements.

You have seen the police and courtrooms in movies, right? Withholding information never goes well.

Case Study: The English Will Of An Italian Heiress

An Italian heiress 'withheld' information from her UK lawyer about her valuable shares in a private Italian company. The UK lawyer, thinking their client's assets were based in the UK, entirely prepared an English Will for the client, including a testamentary trust. This would have been perfect if all the assets were based in the UK.

Unfortunately, it only became clear that this was not the case after the client's demise. The UK testamentary trusts, to the extent they related to the Italian shares, made the Italian tax and succession position very complicated. The English and Italian advisors found themselves basically speaking at cross purposes because that situation had not been anticipated in the lifetime of the testator. Sadly, this meant that the advisers then had to spend years dealing with the Italian tax authorities and the Italian beneficiaries to resolve matters. This is a waste of both time and resources, which could have easily been avoided had the client not 'withheld' information about their Italian shares!

Incredibly, there are situations where even the client themselves may have forgotten that they had an asset in a jurisdiction. Oftentimes it is about assets that they inherited.

For example, in some civil law jurisdictions, there are forced heirship rules, so the client may be entitled to, say, one eighth of a share in a family home in Italy. They are not using it because they themselves live in the UK, and a sibling resides in that home.

So, the client is not even regarding it necessarily as an asset of theirs that requires planning. But it does require planning!

Unfortunately, we see situations like these regularly. Being able to avoid them goes back to how skilful advisers are at communicating with their clients and asking the right questions, as well as how much trust there is between advisor and client.

Many families apply a need-to-know approach to their advisers, with the client becoming the judge of what an adviser needs to know. This is not a strategy that we recommend you follow. If you want the best advice for you and your family, it is essential that you are transparent with your advisors. After all, you are paying them to service your needs based on your specific circumstances!

As advisors, it is essential that we are told the full information; otherwise, our advice may be compromised, with the family finding itself embroiled in a situation that could have been avoided had the full picture been disclosed. For example, there may be inadvertent tax irregularities that arise and need to be corrected to stop them from becoming deliberate non-compliance. The advisor would need to facilitate that happening. How could they do this if there is vital information missing, which would have enabled the issue to be identified early and, even better, prevented mistakes from occurring in the first place? Naturally, the better the questions that an adviser asks of their client, the more likely the adviser is to learn about the bigger picture.

But also, life changes constantly. Children get married, spouses get divorced, family members leave the country to live elsewhere, and sadly people pass away. It is paramount that (anticipated) changes in the family's circumstances are duly communicated to all relevant advisers, as such changes may impact carefully implemented planning to produce unintended outcomes. For example, where a settlor or beneficiary of a family trust moves from a no-tax to a high-tax jurisdiction, it is often too late for the adviser to discover this after the event, as tax consequences are likely to have arisen already. It is essential that regular lines of communication are kept between clients and their advisors throughout.

The quality of the advisor's advice is restricted to the extent and accuracy of the information they are provided with. If you do not trust your advisor with the information that they need you to share, then you should be reviewing your relationship with your advisor and considering replacing them with someone that you do trust.

The word *trust* is vital.

If you do not have trust, there is no relationship between advisor and client. Trust is something that, as we said previously, advisers must earn, and this often comes down to how the adviser builds a relationship with their client. This requires that, as advisers, we understand and communicate the client's values and appreciate that we are merely the guide of their hero's journey. An excellent advisor will also park their ego to one side every time they deal with the client.

Very often, advisors stress their technical competence. But clients expect competence from any decent advisor in their field of professional expertise.

Instead, what is extremely important in building a relationship with the client and earning their trust is emotional intelligence, the ability to put yourself in the shoes of different family members and appreciate the different personalities and perspectives that they bring. In fact, that is how the skilled adviser facilitates dialogue - by being able to see issues from the perspective of the senior generation but also from the perspective of the next generation. An emotionally intelligent adviser can bridge the gap between the two where one exists and support the family itself to work on establishing and opening the channels of communication and engaging more openly with each other.

Your thoughts:

- *Have you ever been in a situation whereby someone deliberately withheld information from you? Information that might have made a significant positive difference had you known?*

Getting The Whole Picture

As advisors, we have a responsibility to obtain a complete picture of the family's assets, circumstances, and tax, regulatory and other considerations. In fact, we would be negligent in our services to the client if we did not. To ensure this happens, communication with the family's advisors, wherever they happen to be based in the world, is essential.

We are responsible for placing the client's needs above everything else, yet how can we achieve this if we do not fully understand the factual matrix? To do so, we rely on the client to share all relevant information, but it may not always be obvious what is and is not relevant. To bridge this gap, advisers need to not only ask insightful questions of their clients but also proactively raise the need for communications to extend to their clients' entire professional teams.

We find it staggering how few professional advisors communicate with all their clients' advisory teams – especially when their clients' assets and family members are scattered across the globe.

What does it take for families to be comfortable with such all-party/all-adviser communications? Fundamentally, it all boils down to the issue of trust – trusting that advisers have the family's best interests at heart; that resultant professional costs will be value for money and not escalate in an uncontrolled way; that all advisers are in it together with the family to promote its unity, the longevity of its family businesses and the protection of its capital in all its forms - and advisers earning that trust.

Ideally, you should have all your advisors sitting with you around the same table at least once a year and addressing issues holistically. We call this the AGM (Annual General Meeting) of professional advisors.

Once an investment manager asked, 'Who should be writing the family constitution?'

Our invariable recommendation is that all the family members should contribute to the shape of the constitution in order that it represents the family's collective vision. After all, it will be the one document that defines the family's purpose and values, as well as provides the framework within which all family decisions will take place in the future. If the family's objective is for all the family members to choose to be bound by the constitution, then it must be formulated with all the family members participating.

On the advisory side, it is usual for a governance expert, whether a lawyer or another professional, to facilitate discussions within the family. These typically start with one-on-one conversations with the individual family members to help the adviser identify issues that have the potential to become a source of discord between them if unaddressed before progressing to all-inclusive roundtable discussions with the whole family at which family consensus can be built, strengthened and brought to a conscious level.

A mistake that families sometimes make is to seek to be very prescriptive in their constitutions and provide for the 'what if's' on a micro-level by reference to their current assets. Because the aim of the family constitution is to provide a cross-generational framework for continuity and an enduring family legacy that may not in the future be defined by the snapshot of assets that the family owns and manages today, it is important that this be a principles-based document that can serve and guide the family over the long term.

Having said that, governance principles elicited by the family as part of the constitution-writing process then feed into every sphere of the family's life. The identification of the family's purpose and values leads to discussions around how they should translate into an impactful strategy. Once the road ahead has been mapped out, families turn to the implementation of their strategic vision - the allocation of time and capital to identify suitable investments and philanthropic projects that deliver on it; resourcing and the recruitment of talent who is not only competent but whose values align with the family's and fit culturally. In time, the issue of succession to roles and assets assumes more immediate relevance. Thus, you can see how the family constitution, being a principles-based document that sets out the family's approach to decision-making as a family, ultimately feeds into the micro-level decisions that the family faces at any given moment in time; but it does not purport to define upfront the specific solution for every eventuality.

Because of this, in answering the question of who should be involved in the creation of the family constitution and governance conversations as a whole, our recommendation is that the wider the circle of professional experts that the family can draw on, the more likely they are to achieve a document that is perceived as fair and reflects the priorities of all family members, irrespective of their personal priorities - on investing, educating the next generation, philanthropy, etc.

Ideally, all the relevant experts in the family's professional team should be invited to contribute to the legal, financial and tax aspects of the family's governance rulebook. Simply having a lawyer draft or review the family constitution can have a limiting effect. For example, they may not be the right person to guide the family on how decision-making for a values-driven investment strategy that embodies the vision of the family should be carried out or to comment on the principles that the family may wish to adhere to when seeking to balance tax efficiency, with social and corporate responsibility and reputational considerations.

The more different perspectives that the family can incorporate into its overall governance and day-to-day decision-making processes, the more likely that they will have something that is really working for them and likely to succeed.

Advisors are key to that conversation.

As an adviser, you may receive information from your client, but this may not necessarily be the full information. A specialist advising purely from the perspective of their domestic law may not appreciate that there are technical nuances that mean their advice can have a detrimental effect on the tax or succession position in another jurisdiction. Or it may be that the specialist who is advising on, say, the Italian succession aspects has access to a different piece of the jigsaw, which is missing from your understanding of the situation.

To address this, we are, once again, going back to that one word – *communication!*

This is not just between the family members but also between the family members and their advisors and indeed between the different advisors to provide a total solution that meets the family's vision, whatever that may be.

Advisors And Agendas

There can sometimes be an issue in families receiving the best advice for their needs where advisors are being protective of their territory and are not necessarily willing to engage with other professionals. That is a clear case where advisors are doing a disservice to the family. If a family is working with advisors like that, they need to understand that such advisors are not working for the benefit of the family but for their own.

There can be an immense benefit to the family receiving integrated advice, typically achieved by having regular meetings with all their relevant advisers in attendance to ensure they all have a complete picture and are not advising in a vacuum.

One of the services that Family Prosperity provides, via the Charles Group, is an annual general meeting (AGM), whereby clients can sit down with all their advisors, literally at a round table! Such an annual meeting of clients and advisors places emphasis on each advisor being held accountable for meeting the family's vision.

A great professional advisor loves being held accountable. It gives them a platform to showcase their expertise to their clients and add value, including by being part of a holistic solution.

If an advisor is not aligned with the family's vision or has an alternative agenda, it is a great time to find this out immediately!

It is essential to uncover which of your professional advisors have a genuine interest in ensuring that the family thrives across multiple generations and the right skillset and motivation to help deliver that. You do not want to wait for five, ten, or 20 years to discover or unearth the motives of each advisor. You need to find out at the earliest opportunity and deal with it accordingly; otherwise, it can become a very expensive mistake.

Some fantastic solutions can come from the family members and their different advisors all sitting at that table. Bringing together smart and emotionally intelligent people to work together to bring about the family's vision is the best investment you can possibly make as a family.

Each professional has their vantage point. They look at the family's circumstances and ambitions from the perspective of their professional expertise, but that is limited to a particular area. If you bring all these experts around the same table, then something entirely different can be born. Two plus two is not four; it can be significantly more.

Great minds can think alike, and there is value to be gained from hearing another adviser's alternative perspective; one thing is clear - the greater the number of great minds that you have in one room, the better the chance of a great outcome. The real benefit is when advisors share their different perspectives and broker solutions collectively that meet the stated long-term needs and priorities of the family. That is just common sense.

Unfortunately, not every advisor sees it that way.

Your thoughts:

- *Does your professional team have your family's best interests to heart, and are they able to work collaboratively with the family and the rest of its advisory team?*

- *Does it not make sense to make your professional advisory team accountable for meeting your family's vision for the future?*

- *Is there any reason why you would not want your advisory team, the best minds, to meet up with you collectively once a year to provide your family with synergistic gains, and help you successfully implement strategies, including for the establishment of your family's legacy?*

- *How often does your family, including the next generation, meet up to discuss the current professional advisory team and who the best contact is?*

Focus On The Whole Family

It can be incredibly valuable to families where the advisor is not only, or predominately, focused on their primary client but on the family as a whole. This allows them to become the family advisor and not just the advisor of the matriarch or patriarch, and for their accumulated knowledge of the family to support and benefit the next generation at the point of transition and beyond.

There is an interesting dichotomy here because as a lawyer or as an accountant, an adviser will have their engagement letter addressed to whoever their client of the record is, and so that is who their duty is owed.

However, in a governance context, whilst it may be that an adviser is engaged by the senior generation, for their advice to be meaningful, it must incorporate the perspectives of the next generation. This is because for the senior generation's vision to survive the generational transfer, the next generation must feel that it is not just their parents' vision but also their own. If the next generation is not involved in these conversations, then there is a very real chance that they will argue over their inheritance, structures they do not understand the rationale for, as well as the control of and strategy for family businesses, and potentially end up in very destructive (of family and wealth) litigation.

Sadly, in families who fail to plan for succession and disregard the need for participative governance, this is a pattern that will often occur until the wealth dissipates.

If there is no continuity, we go back to the shirtsleeves to shirtsleeves in three generations cycle.

Looking after your client - if that is the senior generation, mother and father - also involves opening the discussion to incorporate the next generation. In no other area is this more important than in the context of family governance.

Very often, we witness that because advisors have not built a relationship with the next generation, as soon as mother and father pass away, they feel almost compelled to find their own advisors because they do not have that relationship. If they do not know and trust the advisor, then why should they continue working with them

This may seem like common sense, but many professional advisors miss this fundamental point.

A professional who has been the senior generation's trusted adviser over an extended period of time has what we call institutional memory. So, when the mother and father are not there, being able to tap into the advisors' knowledge of the family from the perspective of both the senior and, in time, rising generations is a vital component of preserving the family's legacy. Yet the next generation cannot be expected to appreciate this fact if it is not communicated to them, including through how the adviser's relationship with the wider family has been conducted.

Unfortunately, when the next generation moves on to new advisors, they start from scratch. That institutional memory, that 'know-how' as to how the family does things, is gone. That is why it is important for there to be a relationship between advisers and the next generation, which is nurtured and fostered whilst the parents are still there.

From the perspective of ensuring continuity for the family, how can an adviser hope to be facilitating the family's governance conversation on the transition from one generation to the next if, until then, their discussions have been limited to those with the senior generation?

The adviser's objective must always be to build ongoing trust and rapport with the family as a whole. This should enable the next generation to rely on the existing professional advisers for support and guidance during what can be an unsettling period of the change of guards. For this to happen, advisers need to have been having conversations with the next generation during their parents' lifetimes and demonstrate through their advice that they are there to help the entire family, including by mediating the different generations' perspectives to build coherence and family consensus.

Statistically, there is only a seven percent chance of the next generation sticking with an existing advisor where no relationship has been built with them over the lifetime of their parents.

If professional relationships (whether with lawyers, financial advisors, accountants, tax advisors, investment managers, trustees, etc.) are to be transitioned successfully, it is vital for advisers to have built that long-ranging rapport with the next generation. When done well, advisers will have earned themselves the 'right' to continue the client relationship with the next generation and the privilege to remain part of their onward journey.

Ultimately, an adviser involved in the family's governance conversations is able to add significant value because not only are they advising from the perspective of their professional expertise, but they have been intimately involved with the family's inter-generational circumstances.

The real forward-looking family chooses advisors based on who their children would feel comfortable taking advice from.

Often, there is even an age component. They may choose an advisor who is partway between the senior and next generation and able to act as a bridge between them - smoothly interfacing between their different perspectives during the parents' lifetimes and providing stability and consistency when they are not there.

Advisors are very rarely chosen by accident. There is a lot of thought that goes into that relationship, and an adviser's competence is only one part of that.

Emotional intelligence and how an adviser fits in within the family's demographics and inter-personal dynamics, as well as how they can work with and integrate the different family members, will typically be front of mind for a family who appreciates the value of family governance and the role of trusted advisers within it.

Tax Advice Is NOT The Key Driver

The next statement may come as counter-intuitive, coming from two professional advisors specialising in tax and succession planning, with more than thirty-five years of experience between us; however, having spoken with many advisors, we believe it should not be too controversial amongst family governance experts, who almost universally will agree with it.

Tax is *not* the key driver!

We would readily acknowledge that tax is important in the context of succession and asset protection. Effective tax planning can minimise and manage tax exposure, which can help maintain the family's wealth in the long run.

However, it is essential to not allow tax planning alone to drive the succession plan and distract the family from what is truly important to them by allowing tax advisors and tax objectives to kidnap the family's asset-holding and succession structures. Sadly, and we are not alone in this, we have witnessed a remarkable number of situations where the senior generation has worked so hard to achieve secrecy and ended up leaving their assets in a messy labyrinth of opaque structures which has facilitated theft, abuse and a legacy of mistrust and unresolved tax liabilities for the next generation to sort out.

It is important that any tax planning and the establishment of tax and trust structures are used to help the family achieve its long-term vision, whatever that may be, in an efficient manner. It is also essential that there is a cascade of family members who are privy to all relevant information and have taken on the responsibility of communicating with relevant advisors on the happening of certain events so that these structures and their associated costs are clearly understood by the family as a whole and there is the handover of knowledge necessary to ensure that they are reviewed and adapted in the light of the family's changing circumstances.

To reiterate, tax planning is a tool and should never be the main driver for legacy planning.

PART 6

Planning Defensively

Expect Disputes If ...

The key theme is, once again, communication. We are assuming professionalism and competence.

We are often asked, what action should families take now to avoid disputes at a future date?

Planning, preparation, transparent discussions, and regular reviews of the plan. It is not a single magic ingredient. Families really need to look at where they are today candidly.

Very often, it is a matter of having those difficult or uncomfortable conversations. Ideally, they can be facilitated through impartial, trusted advisors; because the fish in the water does not have the ability to take a step back and look at it as an observer, they are already swimming in it.

Oftentimes, it will be an externally facilitated discussion with the individual family members before reporting back to the family that enables families to appreciate where potential pressure lines might be emerging; and bring them into an open forum where they can be discussed and diffused or resolved.

Working on being clear about what the family's core values are is critical to maintaining its cohesion and unity across multiple generations, as is an agreed vision about what living those values would look like in practice. This may involve the creation of a philanthropic foundation or project or implementing a values-based investment and business strategy that rallies the family around shared goals.

In any event, the family's vision needs to be inspiring for the next and future generations.

It needs to displace the idea that wealth is just about the individual; creating a purpose greater than the individual means identifying something for the family to aspire to that is much bigger than the individuals that make up the family.

For business families, the family business is going to be a huge focal point. But it may not always be sufficient, as the example of the Ambani brothers shows.

It is key for families to explore the expectations, hopes and aspirations of the next generation. How does the senior generation prepare the leaders of tomorrow and equip them to be those leaders? It is about looking at the business in a longer-term way and acting today to future-proof it.

For example, COVID has been a catalyst for families reassessing their priorities, both for themselves and their businesses. With greater awareness of their own mortality, families have been intent on updating their structuring and estate planning, looking at the succession to roles, as well as planning for business continuity and leadership succession before it becomes imminent.

There are a lot of new themes also coming into that conversation. Technology and ESG are but two of them.

For example, ESG considerations are dominating the thinking of socially conscious, values-driven next generations, who want their wealth to make a difference. As part of that, they are questioning whether the family business, as it is currently operated, is what they would like to be part of, likewise of the family's investment strategies.

Embracing change and even letting the next generation spearhead it may be what the future viability of some of those family businesses, even in the next five to ten years, will depend on. This is because ESG-centric regulation itself will be shifting businesses towards a different model of working. Businesses now need to be environmentally friendly, reduce their carbon footprint and gear towards social responsibility. ESG is no longer in the alternative "bucket" but fast becoming the norm, with companies that display good corporate and social responsibility being more likely to command premium prices for their products and services, as well as in terms of business valuations.

For business families today, emerging themes like these will be filtering through into family conversations that should be taking place today in preparation for what the next generation might want to do tomorrow. They may also provide the context for families crystallising a new purposeful visit that is larger than their individual members.

Prevention Or Else Cure

We doubt anyone would be inclined to question this one!

Obviously, prevention is so much better than cure.

The reality is that the earlier families engage with the processes we have described in this book, the sooner the family members can be brought together within a unified vision that is communicated and accepted inter-generationally.

The earlier those discussions can take place, the earlier there is clarity about what family members are seeking to achieve, who is on board (with which part), what expectations there are and how things can be accomplished in practice.

Prevention easily outweighs finding a cure.

Not only is the cure less effective, but it also tends to be very expensive. Financially expensive, emotionally expensive, time expensive, and it has the capacity to ruin the family relationship permanently.

When we speak of finding a cure, this usually means dealing with discord that has arisen between the family members, often leading to destructive litigation – between siblings, the businesses they run, beneficiaries and the trustees of family structures. These family arguments, regardless of whether they are resolved in the public domain through costly and reputation-destroying litigation, rarely result in a winner.

A family and its relationships are like a beautiful and expensive vase. Once the argument ends up in court, you have, figuratively speaking, dropped the vase; once it smashes into pieces, no matter how well you glue the pieces back together, the cracks will always remain visible, and the structure will have been weakened.

Ironically, while we can easily predict these potential outcomes merely by looking at what the family is doing today to preserve all its financial, human and intellectual wealth, our experience is that families are often unwilling to contemplate them despite the tell-tale signs.

Many families do not appreciate that divisive issues often start in the minutiae of everyday life, which is often treated as trivial by comparison to the seemingly more pressing business or investment decisions that the family must deal with, *'Not important now; just focus on ....'*

Then there are those families who, for a quiet life today, would not address the elephant in the room. When it becomes impossible to ignore, at best, we see an imperfect solution emerge, where the focus is on damage limitation rather than seeking to resolve creatively from the position of generations, siblings, and families coming together in a commitment to positively engage with each other.

As advisers, it is important that we convey to the family how important prevention is and, as part of providing the very best of client care, support them in making it their mantra and acting accordingly. Waiting for the family dynamic to implode is never a good strategy and both the family's and their advisers' commitment must be to prevent this from happening with everything within their power.

Normalcy bias is one of the biggest problems faced by wealthy families today – the perception that because everything is okay currently, everything will always be okay. *'Since everything is OK today, we do not need to spend time and resources putting in place structures and governance because our family will always get on.'* In fact, the best time to implement family prosperity strategies and plans is when the family relationships are still healthy.

Unfortunately, normalcy bias can be a very costly misconception. This can be seen particularly for first generation families, where one exceptional individual controls the family business and the wealth that keeps the family together. The problem always occurs when this person passes away, as it causes a major vacuum, which the family has not planned for or anticipated.

Yet why do the first generation assume they will live forever? Or is it simply a matter of them not wanting to face their own mortality?

The answer, we have discovered, is that it is a little bit of both.

Founders tend to believe that because their family is harmonious today, it will be the same forever. This is naive in many cases, especially when there is a vast amount of money and assets in the equation.

Very often, the potential issues are already present. However, it is the strength of personality of the first generation that tends to bind the family and prevents the cracks from becoming fractures during their lifetime. But the quality of the underlying relationships is already being impacted.

Thus, the genesis of family conflict usually starts when that exceptional individual is still around, but because at that stage, the family operates on a business-as-usual basis and there is strong leadership in place, the family can continue pulling together in the same direction, and the issues remain hidden. That cohesive relationship often disappears when the person that held it together passes away. A vacuum emerges, and if there is no clear plan, no clear leadership and no clear direction, the issues that have been building over time explode quickly, in a very disruptive and expensive way.

This is predictable and avoidable.

Statistically Speaking

We have tried to cover some of the key topics and issues we have experienced as advisors working with wealthy families.

Issues that have shaped our knowledge and expertise.

Family prosperity is a topic we both feel passionate about, and, in the spirit of professional collaboration, we wanted to share our combined knowledge and experience of working with families, including those who still needed convincing that preparing sooner will protect the accumulated assets for generations to come.

Sadly, this is a significant issue for many wealthy families.

The challenges discussed in this book can be avoided, and we wanted to share our recommendations and practical solutions based on our professional expertise.

We have witnessed countless families self-destruct through emotional conflict and, quite simply, we do not want this to happen to your family.

The amount of wealth is irrelevant.

We have come across fathers and sons who destroy their relationship over one property and have highlighted the story of the Chadha brothers, who shot and killed each other over an argument about the family estate that was worth $10 billion.

It is concerning that despite the incredibly accurate and informative long-term studies carried out worldwide, families still continue to be afflicted by these problems.

Statistically, and this figure is worth repeating, 70% of the family wealth will fail within two generations. That percentage climbs sharply beyond 90% when the wealth reaches three generations. This is a sad, damning statistic, and, unfortunately, it is the reality.

Our responsibility as advisors is to ensure that we help our family clients to avoid becoming another damning statistic.

Normality bias is a key driver of that statistic. We hear families say, *'We are a harmonious family!'* Yes, you may be today, but what about tomorrow? If you fail to plan, then you are planning to fail.

Communication within the family is crucial for the long-term success of that family. It is regrettable, but for families who have already experienced unresolved conflict, it may be too late for that conversation to be happening on a whole family basis, as much of the trust that families share has been eroded.

Families need to ask themselves, *'Where is the family today? What is our vision for the future of the family's wealth and has this vision been clearly communicated to and agreed upon by the family members? Does this vision inspire them to follow it? Has the next generation been empowered to contribute to it, including making decisions that will continue to financially benefit the family?'*

The irony is that the best time to speak as a family is when things are going well, when family members are prepared to talk to one another from a position of trust. The best time to act is now.

Do not wait for something to go wrong and then struggle to find a cure. Do not leave your family's legacy to chance!

Start communicating and stop worrying about what may be perceived as sensitive subjects. Provided such conversations are approached with genuine openness and appreciation for what different generations can bring – for what the senior generations have achieved and rising generations can contribute if inculcated with the family's values, inspired by the family's vision and supported to become the leaders of tomorrow (within or outside the family's businesses or structures) – nothing can benefit the family more than opening the channels of communication and then practising using them regularly. Leaving issues to grow due to fear of the reaction that you might get discussing them only creates a problem for tomorrow. If a modicum (and hopefully more) of trust is there between the family members, then the time to act is now.

Do not wait for someone significant within the family context to die, and never leave your family legacy to guesswork or conjecture.

Conclusion

If there is one good thing that COVID has taught us, it is that we need to act now.

We are in an age where information is moving at the speed of light. It has never been easier to make and lose money quickly. Currently, the quickest recorded bankruptcy was a personal fund that went from $10 billion to zero in less than five days!

We do not know what is going to happen tomorrow. We do not have a crystal ball. If you value your family and want to maintain a legacy that survives and thrives for multiple generations, it is vital that you act today.

Our personal message is simple: you are not alone!

We appreciate that certain conversations are difficult to have, and this is where trusted advisers come in - to help facilitate those conversations.

Effective communication is the foundation on which to grow individually and as a family and build your family legacy. Once effective and transparent communications are taking place, you can build on it by creating an inspiring vision that the family members are motivated to follow, adopting sound governance processes, engaging in sustainable philanthropy, and setting up your family bank to augment the family's human and intellectual capital.

These elements are at the heart of maintaining harmony and preserving the family's wealth across generations. And, of course, remember to hold an annual meeting with your advisory team.

Leaving the future of your family to chance and *hoping* for the best is not a strategy we would recommend. Yet this is exactly what many families do, and this is why 70% fail financially within just two generations, and more than 90% fail within three.

You have worked so hard to create a family business or preserve the family wealth that was handed down to you that you expect it to last in perpetuity; you have built up or helped maintain significant wealth so that your children and their children will not have to struggle as you or your predecessors did.

You and your family's current and future generations deserve to be able to benefit from this legacy.

Now is the time to implement the right strategy to ensure that your family legacy thrives for multiple generations.

For further information about how to implement the *Four Fundamentals of Family Prosperity*, we kindly ask you to visit our website *www.familyprosperity.com*.

About Nicholas Charles

Nicholas Charles FCCA is a generational wealth expert, author, property investor, tax expert and a member of the Family Firm Institute (FFI). Nicholas started his journey in family prosperity to create a paradigm shift in family wealth legacy planning. His purpose is to help families understand the business of being a family.

Author of the Amazon number 1 best-selling book The Four Fundamentals of Family Prosperity. Generational Wealth was the follow up book and was first released in October 2022 and managed to get the number 1 spot on Amazon.

Nicholas specialises in family prosperity advice, tax planning and asset protection. For over 20 years he has managed to build up a network of the world's leading professional experts in niche fields including business coaches, lawyers, fiduciaries, technology experts, tax advisors, private banks and wealth managers.

Growing up as second generational wealth with a family that also suffered from generational financial failure, Nicholas became inspired to help families across the world to retain and grow their wealth for multiple generations. Realising the limitations of time and reach as a consultant, Nicholas sought to create a solution using technology that could expand his reach to families across the planet.

A global problem required a global solution. At the beginning of 2023 Nicholas began building a team of technology experts. With his design and their technological expertise, they built a secure operating system for Ultra High Net worth individuals and family offices to help them to digitise generational wealth. This exciting and revolutionary idea grew to become DANTI – the secure operating system that will revolutionise and digitise generational wealth. Nicholas is the co-founder and CEO of Danti Global Limited.

Connect with Nicholas Charles on LinkedIn

https://www.linkedin.com/in/nicholascharles1/

About Antoaneta Proctor

Antoaneta advises on international tax and evaluation of tax risk, cross-border succession, structuring for wealth preservation, and family governance. She acts for (ultra) high net-worth individuals and their families (both UK and non-UK domiciled), entrepreneurs, family offices and trustees, typically with complex and multi-jurisdictional legal needs. Her practice is truly international, with clients coming from backgrounds as diverse as Russia, Israel, Switzerland, South Africa, and the Middle East.

She advises on onshore and offshore trust structuring, Family Investment Companies and the institutionalisation of family offices. A significant area of expertise for her is the preservation and nurturing of family wealth through consultative assessments of the pressure lines and the creation of Family Constitutions.

Antoaneta is a skilled technician, focusing on tax planning and tax regularisation work. She is frequently asked to carry out risk reviews of existing structures from a combined tax and asset protection perspective and assist with remedial work in relation to legacy issues.

Antoaneta is also ideally placed to support trustees in developing checklists and protocols for managing institutional risk in connection with UK-related structures.

Clients value Antoaneta's sophisticated understanding of their needs and aspirations and the ability to maintain both empathy and professionalism throughout.

Praise for Anoaneta Proctor and Chambers & Partners

'She is extremely technically good; I cannot praise her technical ability enough. Her manner with clients is fantastic. She is very down to earth; she does not overcomplicate things, and she always strikes the right tone.'

'What stands out about her is how thorough she is. Her briefing documents are exceptional. You can really tell that she really thinks about the client's needs, and her advice is always in a digestible format.'

Contact Antoaneta Proctor
https://familyprosperity.com/team/antoaneta-proctor

Do You Want To Take The Next Steps To Establish Your Family Legacy?

Please visit our latest website or simply follow us on YouTube or LinkedIn to discover how you can digitise your generational wealth. We regularly post blogs and videos to keep you updated on the latest in generational wealth and legacy planning.

Remember, three strikes and you are out! 90% of families will lose everything in just three generations.

You and your family deserve to build a wealth legacy that thrives for multiple generations.

Do not rely on hope for your generational wealth strategy.

DANTI
Digitising Generational Wealth

Web Address: *www.danti.io*

Danti YouTube page *https://www.youtube.com/@Danti_io/videos*

Danti LinkedIn page *https://www.linkedin.com/company/dantiglobal*

www.ingramcontent.com/pod-product-compliance
Lightning Source LLC
Chambersburg PA
CBHW031406180326
41458CB00043B/6632/J